D0387840

SPOTTED
IN FRANCE

SPOTTED
IN FRANCE

BY GREGORY EDMONT

ILLUSTRATIONS BY MARK REYES

THE LYONS PRESS
Guilford, Connecticut

An imprint of The Globe Pequot Press

COUNTY LIBRARY
TILLAMOOK, ORE.

914.404 EDMONT $19.95
Edmont, Gregory.
Spotted in France /
x, 230 p. :

• • •

COPYRIGHT © 2003 BY GREGORY EDMONT DE LA DOUCETTE

Illustrations © 2003 by Mark Reyes www.gv1.com

ALL RIGHTS RESERVED. No part of this book may be reproduced or transmitted in any form by any means, electronic or mechanical, including photocopying and recording, or by any information storage and retrieval system, except as may be expressly permitted in writing from the publisher. Requests for permission should be addressed to The Lyons Press, Attn: Rights and Permissions Department, P.O. Box 480, Guilford, CT 06437.

The Lyons Press is an imprint of The Globe Pequot Press.

10 9 8 7 6 5 4 3 2 1

Printed in the United States of America.

DESIGNED BY CLAIRE ZOGHB

ISBN 1-59228-147-8

Library of Congress Cataloging-in-Publication Data is available on file.

For JP

Cormeilles-en-Vexin

Trappes

Paris

Montigny-sur-Loing

Joigny

La Charité-sur-Loire

l'Allier

Les Baux-de-Provence
Saint-Rémy

Montpellier

Grimaud

INTRODUCTION

I wasn't in the market for a dog. I knew my life was missing something . . . I just didn't know what, and hadn't thought of it as something *living*. Let alone living with me. I had moved to Paris for graduate school, barely made it through the grueling French education process, and then, lacking direction and any better plan of action, stayed in France. Out of school, out of work, and an outsider in a very closed society, I was about to return to New York when two Parisian friends, twin brothers with twin dogs, insisted over all objections (how broke I was, how much time I didn't think I had for a pet, how much traveling I'd hopefully be doing once I got some work) that I needed one.

Six weeks of courtship to convince the breeder I was a worthy candidate for adoption, and six hundred borrowed euros later, the liver-spotted Dalmatian named Jarny-Prince du Bois-de-Tanagra, son of the Prince des Cœurs du Bois-de-Tanagra and Charmeuse du Domaine Clix, moved into the larger of the two bedrooms of my Montmartre apartment, the only one in which he'd deign to sleep. His had the view of Paris, and of the pigeon-speckled Place des Abbesses. Thankfully, His Highness did acknowledge the more pronounceable nickname of JP.

The very first day I walked JP around the *quartier*, the world became more intimate with me, almost absurdly so. Not only did bonds with acquaintances intensify, but I also began to attract an entirely new breed of French friends. Locals, who had seemingly never noticed me, began to smile and even approach me when I was with JP. Initially I thought it was the charm that puppies work on people—and it was particularly hard for anyone to ignore JP.

Or maybe it was taken as a sign that I was really here to stay, now that I was building a family. But it seemed to me that it was something more. As one French friend remarked: "You made yourself Parisian. JP made you *French*."

Being Parisian required things like knowing when and when not to laugh (rarely), how and how not to shop (one-small-piece-of-cheese-at-a-time), where and where not to eat (not at the famous places). Being French meant doing all that with a dog.

JP became my golden key to practically every bar, café, and restaurant in Paris . . . and eventually my passport to all of France. Genuine Parisians, those born and raised in the City of Lights, are often not as accepted in the provinces as JP and I were. Doors began to open to me, previously locked doors, those reserved for *les français*.

Animal lovers will tell you things like, "I don't trust anyone who doesn't like animals." Dog lovers in America gravitate toward one another; they share a common bond that often transcends social barriers. I soon discovered that the whole of the French nation is dog loving. The bond between France and me and my dog was instantaneous and profound.

Through JP, I learned that the French pride themselves on their ability to live in harmony with nature: her cycles, her seasons, and her animals (even the ones they eat); it is a fundamental part of their culture. And that what can be seen as arrogance is often nothing more than shyness. The French are threatened by the power of man, especially the non-French man; perhaps after centuries of war and bloodshed, it's bred into them. It is true that while some French consider themselves superior, culturally at least, to other nations, they are humbled by and respectful of nature. Man they buck, nature they don't—they revere and are grateful to her. It somehow seems fair that the most fertile land on the European continent should belong to France, and that it should extend to some of the most exquisite shores of the Mediterranean.

The beauty of the land was apparent from the day I set foot in the country; to discover the true nature of the people, it took an intelligent, handsome, well-mannered dog—one who quickly learned to sport goggles and ride on the footrest of a Vespa scooter, a reflection of the harmony possible between man and animal—to erase the shell of superiority, shyness, and fear and reveal the modesty, kindness, and humor that lie just below its surface.

LE DEPART
FROM PARIS

No CONVINCING WAS necessary. A change of scenery and some extra euros were just what I needed. JP was sitting by the phone, and seemed to react to Madame Clix's heartfelt plea — "I'm truly desperate and I'll pay a generous stud fee" — or maybe he'd overheard her bribe: "JP's destiny is calling him . . . and believe me, he'll enjoy it." A pair of goggles and a paw plopped onto my chest assured me that JP needed it, too, and determined the means by which we would travel. I'd probably have chosen the train.

Some people weigh all the pros and cons before acting; some people just act. JP and I were somewhere in the middle. After two years of cohabitation, we had developed a certain codependent seesawing: I hesitate, take an instinctive cue from him, think again, and *then* act. Given the inevitable nature of a dog's existence in man's world, JP rarely initiated the bouncing of the seesaw, but he took his role in the process very seriously, and he was proud of his ability to tip the scales. I suppose it's because he isn't a man that his instincts have nearly always been right.

"We'll do it," I said. "But . . ."

"Marvelous," Madame Clix said, and hung up, before I could ask why the situation was so urgent, why JP, or how much *generous* meant.

•   •   •

"*S'il vous plaît, Monsieur.* Does he have a leash?" asked the owner of Astrolabe, the best map store in Paris, in an arresting tone as JP and I walked toward her, dog before man. Before I could respond negatively (I hadn't carried a leash since JP was six months old), JP slowed to my pace, positioned himself at my right side, and began to move his legs in perfect sync with mine. When I stopped, JP froze so that his right front paw remained mid-air, mid-step. The woman looked at us with a combination of disbelief and amusement, and shrugged as we reached the register. "Seems he doesn't need one." She held out a biscuit. JP sniffed it, took it gently from her hand, and held it between his teeth, looking small and grateful.

"Can I help you find something?" asked the now thoroughly charmed woman.

"I'd like to map out a scenic route to the south of France," I replied.

"How far south?" she asked.

"All the way," I said. "By scooter."

She gave me a quick once-over, determined that I was serious, and then in typical French fashion displayed no further reaction to the oddity of such a road trip. "Do you happen to need anyone to look after this little man?"

I could feel JP inching imperceptibly closer to me. "Oh, he's coming, too," I said.

This time she couldn't help but raise an eyebrow, and after a thoughtful moment she smiled. "I've got just the thing," she said. "The wet way, so you can stop whenever he gets thirsty. If you're not in a *terrible* hurry to get there." She led me to the section of maps for bicyclists. JP didn't follow, and I decided to leave him to his own flirtatious devices; another employee was eyeing him. JP gave the biscuit to her, and then caught up with us, looking large and bored.

•   •   •

As I lay sprawled out alongside a detailed map of France, which unfolded was practically the length of the living room floor, JP lay in front of it, looking concerned. He was enthusiastic about seeing new places, but less than confident about my sense of direction and my tendency to overplan. The "wet way" was a zigzag route of some five hundred miles along rivers and streams, and the itinerary coincided nicely with the self-made map I'd cut and pasted from country inn guides. It would take a while to get to the breeder, but we had time; the one bit of information Madame Clix had shared with me was that the fiancée to whom JP was now promised wouldn't be *disposée* for roughly another two weeks.

We had to travel light, so I extracted only the pertinent pages of the *Michelin Guide* that we'd need for restaurants along our route and set them on our pile of essentials: two pairs of goggles, two helmets (JP's was really a comfortable leather cap, and both would soon be discarded), two towels, three pairs of underwear, three pairs of socks, two pairs of shorts, one pair of jeans, one proper shirt, one after-shave kit, one bowl, one Armani jacket (black, with white hairs), one rubber ball, one credit card (nearly up to its limit), and one montage of a map (highlighted with inexpensive inns and not-so-inexpensive restaurants).

· · ·

The morning of our departure dawned sunny and warm, perfect for the Vespa. As on the day we had bought it eighteen months prior, JP was the first to hop on. I'd been testing the newer scooter when JP found a vintage model and sat all sixty pounds of himself on its flat footrest, then looked at me as if to say, *Just right.* I looked at the hump in the footrest of the new model, noted the infinitesimal space for my legs on the one JP preferred, and pulled out the credit card. Once again, dog had trumped man. At the time, however, we hadn't intended it for long-distance dog transportation, or at least one of us hadn't.

JP sat patiently on the scooter as I filled the saddle box attached behind the seat. Once I was on, JP stuck his head up and out for the habitual adorning of the goggles to protect his eyes. "He's so cute!" cackled one of the Brazilian transvestites who frequented the alley across from our apartment. "Like father, like son!" She threw her unlikely mop of red hair first forward, then back, and swayed her hips to show how scant her slit skirt was. "If I thought you could afford me, I'd hop on that contraption with you," she continued, revealing a little more leg.

JP kept a respectful distance from *les travelos*, but would always wag a cheery hello. *Les travelos* never failed to greet us *bons voisins* (good neighbors) with a little provocative humor. We didn't voice complaints about their squatting and red-lighty business practices in the vacant building across the street, and in return, the courtyards and windows and balconies of our

Montmartre apartments were never left to the mercy of burglars, *cambrioleurs*, who sometimes targeted our out-of-the-way neighborhood. These girls knew exactly who did and who did not belong on our balcony. They worked in shifts, round-the-clock, so it was like having a twenty-four-hour watch. Only once did I ever see a person dare to mess with them: a dissatisfied client (or perhaps just a perplexed one—from a distance, at least, some of their breasts put other, more natural ones to shame) who had decided not to pay for services already rendered, a decision he barely lived to regret.

"*Bon voyage !*" Denis or Denise waved as I started the motor. JP gave a rapid wag of his white tail and then lifted his body so that I could tuck it under him, between his hind legs, before we rode off.

•   •   •

"No way," I whispered down to JP. Ever the backseat driver, he was pressing his head into my right knee, indicating that that was the direction we should take. Turning right did not look to me to be the easiest way out of Paris. For one thing, the radio had said to avoid driving anywhere near the Ministry of Education. For another, I could see from where we were stopped at the intersection that the rue Grenelle was packed with people, not vehicles.

Horns started blasting urgently behind us, accompanied by desperate shouts: "*Eh ! Bouge-toi ! Qu'est-ce que tu fous là ?*"

What is who *doing?* I wondered. Looking around, I saw that the light was about to turn green. Green lights are one of the few things the French aren't late for.

When the angry driver caught my eye, he screamed *"Beh alors ! Well?"*

I smiled peaceably, which only further infuriated him. He made an obscene gesture and swerved around us.

As the driver passed, however, he saw JP nestled between my legs, and his contorted hand and hellish glare transformed themselves into a wave and the most beatific of smiles, as if he hadn't just wished me dead on the spot. *"Ah ! Quel joli chien !* Pretty dog! Drive carefully with him." JP averted his eyes from the man's and planted his head firmly on my right thigh.

Turning right ended up being the only way to get through France's latest *manifestation* of name-calling, tomato-throwing, banner-bearing demonstrators protesting some cause or another. The intention of the protesting teachers and students was to prevent vehicles from passing, but the approach of this spotted, two-wheeled, begoggled creature caused the opposite result. I marveled at the parting-of-the-Red-Sea effect that JP had.

"Quick! Through here!" shouted a North African student as he stepped back onto the sidewalk to let us pass. "Keep going straight. *Les flics* are blocking the other streets."

It was three-ten in the afternoon, and we made it to the Porte de Sèvres entrance to the *périphérique* at three-fifteen. I later learned that at three-twenty exactly the police had closed the ring road in response to a bomb threat. No other vehicle had exited central Paris by any means until nightfall.

• • •

A couple of hours later, after losing our way only once, we were soaring down a country road along the Oise River. I stopped to take off my helmet so that I could really feel the wind. It felt as though we were flying through the patches of forest, then cornfields, then fields with wild purple and white and yellow flowers like a patchwork quilt. It was as if the land had not been tended, as if it had always been like that, as if no one lived in the small château perched on a hill in the background that stayed with us as the road turned. It felt as if it were ours and ours alone.

JP's head was resting on my knee, and I could feel his muzzle sniffing and twitching contentedly. I closed my eyes (admittedly dangerous, but the road was straight at this point) and just *smelled*. An entirely new sensation. Had I ever even used my nose before? As if sensing my pleasure, or perhaps because of his own, JP looked up at me and stretched to reach my chin with his tongue.

The color began to fade to golden fields of wheat and I was reveling that JP and I were the masters of our universe, that we were the only two souls in northern France, when the road turned and dropped steeply, revealing a farmer, cane in one hand and bell in the other, crossing with his sheep. JP and I skidded to a stop. The farmer halted, and then hobbled toward us, to blast us for speeding, I supposed. But in the bright sunlight he just squinted at us, and through the slits I saw piercing gray eyes cornered by deep lines, like gouges almost, cut into the unnaturally smooth, rosy skin of an elderly man's face. His eyes seemed to say that he knew something very important that I didn't, and self-consciously I looked away.

The sheep began to gather around him, and we found ourselves surrounded by dozens of confused, baaa-ing, smelly masses of white. JP sat in a questioning but blasé position (nothing really fazes him), not knowing what to make of them, but following my lead in not reacting. The farmer didn't seem at all nervous about having his sheep in such close proximity to this dog who with one bark could probably have sent the entire flock running for the hills. The sheep, on the other hand, grew increasingly agitated, but the man merely stood watching us in silence for a fairly long while. I suppose I could have been the one to say *bonjour*, but for some reason it didn't seem necessary.

Finally, the man walked behind the scooter, looked at my Paris-coded license plates ending in 75—the first thing most French do when vehicles enter their villages, to determine the provenance, and then scowl or not, depending. He looked at JP's cap, and then at my bare head. He stuck the handle of his bell into his rear pant pocket to free a hand, then took off his own cap (not quite a beret, but almost) and threw it to me like a Frisbee. I raised my hand, but JP lifted his body slightly higher and caught it mid-air. The man nodded his head slowly, not quite smiling, not quite frowning, and said, *"Bravo"* in the matter-of-fact way the

French often pronounce that word: brrrah-*voh*. It was obvious from his nonexpression that the exclamation was because of the ensemble that was JP: a Dalmatian in full gear on a scooter, and a good catcher to boot.

The man turned and walked away as casually as he'd approached, even though his sheep were more upset than ever, scurrying in confused circles. Without looking back (at us or the sheep), he entered a field and shook his bell. The sheep grew silent and followed him, one by one, and two by two. It went without saying that I would extend the courtesy of not accelerating until the last sheep had crossed.

•   •   •

When we arrived at our destination of the Relais Sainte-Jeanne in the village of Cormeilles-en-Vexin, I parked discreetly behind a tree on the grounds. My back ached and my legs were so stiff that I could hardly straighten them when I got off the scooter. JP leapt off and stretched in more directions and positions than I had ever seen him undertake. Twenty-five miles had never seemed so far. I watched JP closely and then, much to his amusement, imitated him. I checked my windblown hair in the mirror and contemplated the futility of trying to comb it. I tried on the cap the farmer had given me. It looked pretty cool, actually.

"*Quelle beauté !*" JP the beauty was the first to be greeted (and the first to be seated, and the first to be served) in the restaurant.

"Fais-moi un bisou !" I think JP is pretty much bilingual. At least I'm sure he understands "give me a kiss" in any language.

As soon as I entered (right behind JP), I felt the soreness in my body fade away, so physical was the aura of serenity. When JP was finished stripping the elegant Madame Cagna, wife of the celebrated chef Gérard Cagna, of her lipstick, and about to attack her blush, she rose, arranged a few stray locks of her platinum-blond hair, and led us into a spacious salon with abundant floral arrangements and candlelight flickering from table to table like bouncing, shooting stars. When the chef approached, JP lost all interest in feminine cheeks and focused on masculine hands.

"I just stuffed a pheasant," the chef said happily enough when I apologized and told JP to stop. JP stopped licking and sat very obediently (and expectantly) in front of his new best friend. "I bet you'd like a bit of that, *pépère*, wouldn't you? Let's see what we can fix you up with." I watched JP's expression. JP had him and he knew it. "Brigitte, put them at seven."

Table number seven was situated in front of a bay window overlooking a rose and lilac garden. One of its two chairs was promptly removed and replaced by its cushion and a bowl of water. Warm, flaky miniature pastries of Roquefort cheese and sun-dried tomatoes were then set down before me.

I looked around the mostly filled dining room from my high-backed, armrested chair in the corner, not really wondering what entitled me to this particular table when there were probably mayors and senators and European personalities at other less desirable ones, merely appreciating it. JP got me good tables in Paris, too.

"The *menu Sainte-Jeanne, s'il vous plaît*," I said, before Madame Cagna could hand me the menu, knowing that the pre-selected choices of the *maison* were what had earned the chef his second Michelin star.

After I had ordered my aperitif and wine, I settled back, opened the book I had packed as an afterthought that morning. I became engrossed in a new chapter, and then in a duo of smoked and marinated salmon with olive oil and lime, a *foie gras* soufflé so light that it melted on my tongue, and *boeuf* Wagyu roasted with black peppercorns.

JP's main course was a small dish of specially prepared chicken broth risotto (all I'd requested was rice) with a side of *fromage frais*. Afterward, JP laid his head upon the former seat cushion and floated off, legs spasmodically trotting, to chase the rabbits and geese needed for tomorrow night's dinner.

As we were leaving the restaurant, Madame Cagna came over, saying she couldn't resist another kiss. In between slobbers, she asked if I was English. When I told her that I was American, she said, "Oh. That explains it. I was wondering about your cap. I suppose it'll be the new style in France next year. You *speak* wonderful French, though."

CHAPTER

2

LIVER IN
TRAPPES

As OFTEN HAPPENS when we travel, I woke up before JP. He was curled up at the firm foot of the bed, sound and comfortably asleep, whereas I was an aching ball, sunken into the pit of the center of the well-used mattress. At the planning stage I'd determined that the only way this gastronomic road trip was going to work financially was if I was prepared to sacrifice good beds for good tables. I was now rethinking the wisdom of that plan.

After shaking JP awake and letting him outside, I guzzled some strong black coffee (even the most modest of French inns won't deprive guests of morning coffee served in the room) and unfolded the patchwork map, laying it out on the floor to see if we might take a star off a restaurant or two and add one to some of the lodgings I'd booked. I used my portable phone to cancel a reservation for that night at the Formule Une (the French equivalent of a Motel 6) and found a two-star hotel not far from it. I was about to make a call to confirm a room when JP walked across the map, puncturing it in the center, the hole practically smack on our final destination. With him staring at me, intensely expressing his desire to hit the road, I decided to play the evening's accommodation by ear.

Securely nestled in his spot on the footrest, his sole purpose in life to be sitting on a Vespa with his ears flapping in the wind, JP was happy again, and I was content to be his driver without any particular destination other than the blue-and-gold horizon and whatever caught our eyes in between. Our detour to Cormeilles-en-Vexin had taken us northeast of Paris, and so we had a few hours of driving south through the *département* of

Yvelines, down to Trappes and then Rambouillet before we would be on the old road to Fontainebleau. The name *Yvelines* signifies "rich in water," and its old water mills dating back to feudal times dotted the small forests and valleys we passed through.

The first break we took was along the Yvette River, upstream, where it is a beautiful deep green, but not murky. While JP waded and drank, I lay down on the grass with a notebook and jotted down random thoughts.

"*Tiens bien la broche, Laridon !* Hold the skewer!" a woman's voice called out softly, startling me. "*Désolée*, young man," said the graying, middle-aged woman to whom the voice belonged. She stood over me and pointed to JP, who was occupied by a giant oak tree, twisting and turning one of its large roots as if determined to extract it from the bank of the river. "Is he in training to be a *tournebroche ?*" she added, laughing.

I half smiled, not getting what she'd meant, never mind who Laridon might be. She frowned and said, "Surely you know that's what Cyrano de Bergerac said to his adversary, comparing him to a poor dog trained to turn a skewer." She looked at me for an answer until I shrugged my ignorance. She squatted, rolled up the cuffs of her loose-fitting cotton pants, and then climbed down the embankment toward JP. "Looks like your dog could use a little instruction, too," she said as she stood in the river, yanked the root out in one swift movement, and handed it to JP, who immediately lost interest and turned away, the claim to the prize no longer his. He refused to play tug-of-war with the woman, despite her insistent prodding—this amused her a bit too much, and I figured that she might not be altogether sane.

"So what kind of writer are you then, if not a fan of Edmond Rostand?" she asked.

"A struggling one," I answered, gathering from her recital of cryptic literary passages that she had a thing for Cyrano de Bergerac, his creator, Edmond Rostand, or maybe just his latest incarnation, Gérard Depardieu.

"You do know at least that Rostand lived up there"—she pointed to a path across the road—"and that he wrote much of his *poésie* in the very spot you've permitted yourself to occupy."

I didn't know whether Rostand had lived in Yvelines, or how she could know where he composed his poetry. "Really?" I asked skeptically, but wanting to believe it.

"The bad news is that you need to brush up on your history," she huffed. "The good news is that fate has brought you here." She smiled, motherly, and said, "You look sad."

Suddenly I did feel sad, because a stranger should find me so, or maybe because I was and just hadn't known it. "That's good for a writer," she continued, seeming slightly saner. "My husband used to write a little. He was a sad creature, too. You should have a look at Rostand's Château de Mauvières. It'll cheer you up. I'd go with you but I sense you'd rather be alone. It's just up the path."

"*Merci*," I said.

"*De rien*," she quipped as she unrolled her pants.

JP strolled up next to her, shook himself off until she was soaked, and then licked her lowered face. "Ah!" she waved him away. "So *now* you want to play! Too late! Go and see the château with your *papa !*"

Just up the path meant trudging a mile through woods and crossing two more roads. Luckily we ran into a couple of walkers who knew how to get there. When we arrived at the early-eighteenth-century castle, we found that it had been rented out for a private wedding. From the gate it didn't look like anything exceptional (as French châteaux go) but JP was happy for the walk, and a gardener proudly confirmed that Rostand had indeed lived there, and had written poetry under an oak tree by the river.

• • •

Excited that fate had seen fit to link Rostand and me, I daydreamed of the possible significance as JP and I flew in the direction of Trappes. My mind was filled with romantic images of my destiny, like feather-pen writing in candlelit niches in turrets, and not at all with practical thoughts such as refueling or the nonexistent state of my writing career. In fact, I shouldn't have been traveling at all, but rather looking for a job. It was as if things were placed precariously on hold, and yet somehow I knew that was as it should be—even when the Vespa coughed and sputtered to a stop a few miles outside of Trappes and JP's unenthused expression reminded me that he'd only just had his afternoon walk and didn't require another.

In the late-afternoon light I could see a few farms scattered across the plain that lay ahead, and so I started to walk in their direction, assuming that JP would follow. Instead he plopped himself on the scooter and closed his eyes. I decided a better idea might be to wait for a passing motorist: Perhaps the truck I could hear rumbling our way from somewhere in the distance would stop. JP feigned sleep as the truck approached, while I waved animatedly to get the attention of the speeding driver. Rather than slowing down, he maneuvered to avoid me and shook his index finger at me scoldingly. He swerved far to the left, onto the gravel shoulder, kicking up a cloud of dust and leaving behind a bale of hay that landed a few inches from my feet. JP got up and shook himself off as I rinsed my stinging eyes with the last of our Evian. I could make out another vehicle approaching, and this time JP stretched lazily in the dead center of the road. I called him, but he only inched in my direction and stared at the slow-moving tractor.

A young girl, sitting on a man's lap, appeared to be driving. When they got close, the man pulled a lever and the tractor screeched to a stop.

"Chloë, my little flea, look at the *beau dalmatien* !" he said as he stepped off the tractor, revealing his full height of something like seven feet. JP went to greet him, barely coming up to his shins. He bent down, picked up the hay, and threw it behind the seat of the tractor. "*Bonjour. Il y a un problème ?*" he asked me.

I explained that I'd run out of gas. He nodded and asked where I was headed, in the informal *tu-toi* that the French employ when addressing contemporaries with whom they presume to share a certain bond, or someone for whom they have no respect.

"Fontainebleau," I answered, not sure if I was a peer or a pauper to him.

"On that?" He laughed, waiting for the reply I decided not to give. "All I've got is diesel with me, but I've got some *essence* at home. Will your dog ride on a tractor?"

We both looked over at the delightedly squealing Chloë. JP had already jumped up and installed himself in the driver's seat next to her and was alternating between licking her face and her lollipop. "*Dis donc,*" the man joked. "Not too friendly, is he, your dog?"

I called out for JP to stop slobbering and the man concurred. "*Oui,* Chloë, don't let him do that . . . *ta sucette* is not good for him. Dogs need to chew, not lick."

Chloë thought about this. "*Ah bon,*" she said, and handed JP the stick end of the lollipop to chew. "*Voilà.*" She smiled. Her father and I laughed, and she looked at me proudly with huge brown eyes. "I'm five," she said.

"That's old," I said.

"No it's not," she corrected me.

"How old is Pongo?" Chloë referred to JP by the name of the famous Disney Dalmatian—in France, JP had become so accustomed to "Pongo" that he would often respond to it.

"He's two!" I called back, one hand holding the rope that towed me, the other trying with much difficulty to keep the handlebar facing forward. JP was much more comfortable, wedged in between Chloë and her father as we bounced over rocks and potholes on a dirt path that cut through a field toward a green patch of forest.

"He's not very old, either!" Chloë observed.

.   .   .

A centuries-old stone farm suddenly appeared from behind the trees. Red and white geraniums lined a walkway and filled a small courtyard where a pretty woman standing at about five feet was pounding a rug against a stone wall. Even though it was warm, smoke was billowing from the chimney. "*Op* !" the man said to Chloë, very loudly so that I could hear. "*Maman* has the fire going . . . that means it's going to rain."

I looked up, but there wasn't a cloud in the sky.

As soon as we came to a full stop, JP jumped off the tractor and went to greet the woman. "Look, *Maman* ! It's Pongo. He's coming to play with us," Chloë said, still very serious.

"Well hello!" the woman said to me. I leaned the scooter against the tractor and walked over. "*Et bonjour, toi* !" she said over and over to JP, smiling brightly, as if she knew him and it were the most normal of things for us to be there. "I have a Vespa. It used to be my aunt's. But I haven't ridden it in years—my husband won't let me. What year is yours?" she asked.

"It's a 'sixty-three. A V-Five-A," I replied.

She swung the rug a last time. "*Non* ! You're joking. So is mine!" she exclaimed.

"No it isn't, Clarisse. Your aunt's is a 'sixty-two," her husband corrected. "And you can ride it anytime you want now that you're not pregnant."

Clarisse looked over at her brand-new Range Rover parked in the driveway. "I guess I have gotten used to four-wheeled transportation," she confessed. "Maybe mine is a 'sixty-two," she added doubtfully, disappointed.

That exchange reminded me that the French are very fatalistic: They want to believe that what most Americans would call chance encounters are actually part of some greater plan, sometimes to the point that they stretch reality. Yet they can also be hair splitters: The difference between 1962 and 1963 was an eternity to her.

The hand of fate also allowed that the walls of Chloë's bedroom—which she insisted on showing to JP and me while her father found some gas—were covered with Dalmatian wallpaper, and that her favorite book—a children's illustrated hardback of *Les 101 Dalmatiens*—was lying open on the floor. Or maybe it was Chloë's destiny that she should come face to face with a real Dalmatian for the first time, since she'd always wanted one. Her room was otherwise flowery, pink and white mostly, with fluffy ruffled bedding on a gilded bed frame, rather ornate, I thought, for a little girl.

Chloë told me to sit down on a miniature chair while she flipped through the pages, explaining how the pictures told the story. Instead I sat on the floor and leaned against it. Suddenly she stopped, staring at one of the pages looking very confused, and asked, "Why are Pongo's spots brown?" Figuring she knew the answer before I could reply, she called out to her mother: "*Maman ! Come quickly!* Pongo is dirty!" Chloë looked at me and smiled understandingly. "Don't worry, *Maman* will wash him."

Instead, Chloë's mother called back, "Well then take him out of your room. That pigsty is dirty enough!"

Chloë shook her head and looked at me. "He's sleeping," she said.

I looked at her bed where JP was pretending to be dead to the world and unbotherable. "He's brown and white because he's a liver-spotted Dalmatian. So he's not dirty . . . but he is very bad to be on your bed," I said, with an emphasis on the word *bad* that caused one of JP's eyes to open.

"He's not bad!" JP stretched and climbed off the bed. "Because he eats liver he's that color," Chloë said decidedly. I smiled and led JP toward the door and out of the room.

Although the farmhouse itself was rustic and needed work here and there, it was furnished with expensive antiques, and part of the floor in the hallway was made of glass, beneath which flowed a stream that led into another room. A floodlight built into the floor illuminated the dark water. I decided that when I had a house some-day it would have to be built over an underground water source.

In the case of this house, Chloë's mother told me, it was by ac-cident: When they inherited the house from her aunt, much of the floor was covered with mold. They tore it up and found a spring slowly making its way through the floorboards, and they made the best of it. "It was either glass floors or a new house," she said.

In the courtyard Chloë's father had already filled the Vespa with *super* with a little extra lead, and said I'd be ready to roll . . . a bit later. A drop of rain fell on my face, and I looked up to see that the sky was now covered over.

"We're okay riding in the rain," I said. "Although maybe not all the way to Fontainebleau."

He frowned. "Rain's not the problem . . . you've got a flat tire. I tried adding air but it's shot."

I was sure that the rocky ride across the field had caused it, but seeing how bald the tire was, I realized it had been an accident waiting to happen. Naturally, the one thing I'd forgotten was a spare.

"Paul, a tire from a 'sixty-two won't fit a 'sixty-three," Clarisse called out from a window.

Paul shrugged. "I don't see why not. I've got to deliver the chickens to the butcher before five, but I'll try and swap the tires after that."

I wondered how it could be so obvious to them that I hadn't another tire—and that I wouldn't be able to change it myself.

"Can I help with the delivery?" I asked.

"You can hold the meat bag if you want," Paul replied, happy, I think, to have a male companion. He led me around the back to a barn where Chloë was just walking out. She was alone, with two bloody hands.

"What have you been up to?" her father asked.

"I was feeding Pongo," she said.

"Feeding him what?"

"Liver, that's what he likes," she said to her father, unapologetic, and then to me: "Isn't that right?"

I nodded, trying not to laugh.

"*Merde*," Paul swore.

"I'm telling you said that," Chloë whispered, shocked, and ran to find her mother.

JP stopped feasting as we entered, rolling over on his back as if expecting a belly rub, looking innocent. He had devoured not only an entire bag of raw chicken livers and other innards, but two whole, freshly beheaded chickens as well.

"My brother-in-law has no business sense, couldn't negotiate a flea off your dog's back, so he drops *le poulet* off here and I see the butcher about a good price," Paul said, seemingly exasperated with both JP and his sister's husband.

"I'm really sorry," I said. "I suppose the whole lot is ruined." There were still about a dozen chickens on ice in a metal bin.

"*Mais non.*" He shrugged. "He might have licked a few, but they're all getting cooked anyway." He reached for a large, vinyl bag and handed it to me. "Here, please, hold this open." He proceeded to throw all but two of the remaining chickens into the bag, along with a few chunks of ice, twisted the bag shut, slung it over his shoulder, and, with a free hand, stroked JP's belly. "No big deal, *pépère.*"

Paul left, and I glared at JP, who rolled back over and sat up, looking guilty.

•   •   •

Although it tasted good, Clarisse's dinner of licked, roasted chicken with a salad of shredded carrots and mayonnaise, served with a nice Chinon, was less appetizing than it could have been:

JP, bloated and gassy, was lying by the table, occasionally moaning, ignoring the small dish of half-cooked rice and nettles (for his upset stomach) that Clarisse had prepared for him. I suggested that he go outside, but Chloë wouldn't hear of it. She played with her bits of chicken until Clarisse told her she could lie down beside JP. Chloë stroked his head, distressed that she might have caused him to feel ill but giggling about the gas, until they both fell asleep on Chloë's *couette*, the Dalmatian blanket she carried from room to room.

Clarisse served homemade *tarte Tatin* for dessert. She poured heavy cream onto the plate around my portion (without asking if I wanted any) but none around her own or Paul's. We ate in a comfortable silence until Paul began to nod off at the table. Clarisse stood up softly and motioned for me to as well. Unlike Paul, JP and Chloë instantly woke up, and Clarisse led the three of us to the parlor—another room where we could see the river flowing beneath us—for a *digestif*. This time JP and Chloë found one of the sofas to sleep on. Clarisse indicated a cushiony high-backed chair for me.

Clarisse's family was in the Calvados business, and she was adamant that I should have a taste of Normandy's best—something to offset the red wine and perk me up—before JP and I hit the road. She poured us each a glass and settled into her own sofa across from me. It was getting late, and I was anxious about the road ahead of us, but Clarisse was determined to continue her hunt for the fateful reason I'd ended up in her parlor; it seemed that she'd given up on the Vespa connection.

She soon found what she was looking for: The aunt from whom she'd inherited this farmhouse had fallen in love with a soldier from Connecticut during World War II. To Clarisse, Connecticut was practically Massachusetts, which happened to be my home state (red wine and Calvados can cut through the split hairs). We clinked glasses to our paths crossing.

She looked over at JP and Chloë and smiled. "Life is strange," she said meaningfully, and then focused on some object in the distance and slipped into a quiet, reflective space. I sipped my Calvados and floated away myself.

• • •

I thought about another chance meeting I'd once had: the conversation at a café in Montmartre that led me to JP. I was at a crossroads, with graduate school, and the job in Paris that had helped finance it, both finishing at the same time. I was idle, and a little depressed, just another starving writer in Paris—and I in particular am not someone meant to go hungry. Deep in contemplation, I think I actually uttered the words "What now?" aloud.

"*Une bière*, maybe?" suggested a bohemian Montmartre type with a ponytail, faded jeans, and a threadbare foulard around his neck; a Belgian shepherd sat by his side. "You look like you could use one." He signaled to the bartender to bring two drafts.

I was more surprised that a Parisian—bohemian or not—was initiating a conversation with me than by his dog, who was trying to crawl into my lap, undeterred by the cramped space and un-hindered by her owner.

"Ilène likes you. I saw that immediately when we walked in," he said. "*Et je m'appelle* Laurent," he added.

After a few minutes of what I thought was casual chitchat—mostly Laurent asking me about myself and what I was doing in Paris, and me avoiding the nosier questions, and eye contact, by caressing Ilène's soft coat—he boldly told me that I was a bit self-absorbed, and asked if I had ever thought about getting a dog.

"I don't even know where my own meals will be coming from—never mind feeding another mouth," I said, probably not doing a very good job at hiding my irritation at his observation.

"See what I mean?" he said, and smiled.

"I don't believe it," said a duplicate of Laurent who approached, staring at Laurent's dog. "Ilène normally hates everyone," the clone went on, astonished that the dog had her head on my knee and was allowing me to caress her. Laurent's twin brother, Florent, came with his own Belgian shepherd named Irène, who trailed loyally behind him.

"*Oui*, that's why we're sitting here. I was just telling Greg that he needs a dog," Laurent said. A look of revelation came over their two faces as they pronounced two words in sync: "Madame Clix."

·   ·   ·

"Do you think he still has a chance at playing professional basketball in America?" Clarisse's voice brought me back to the present, and I looked up to see the giant figure of Paul in the doorway. "I mean, he's only thirty-six."

Paul smiled lovingly. "Only!" he said in mock exasperation.

"He thinks he's old—but I know it's never too late to follow your dreams," she said.

Paul responded a bit shortly: "You worry about following your own dreams and I'll worry about mine."

Clarisse changed the subject quickly by asking me if it was true that when Americans meet you, the first question they ask is how much money you earn in a year. I said that I'd been working up the nerve to pop the question all through dinner. They both laughed. Paul stretched, making himself look even taller, and her even smaller, and sat down beside her. Clarisse poured a glass of Calvados for Paul, and refilled mine.

"One more for the road," she said. "I'm sure my Vespa's a 'sixty-three."

Paul waved his index finger in a negative motion. "*Ehn. Ehn,*" he said, and kissed her on the forehead.

"Anyone knows a tire from a 'sixty-two wouldn't fit a 'sixty-three, not a V-Five-A," Clarisse retorted, as she corked the bottle of Calvados. I didn't know, but I would find out a year later that she was right.

MORE LIVER
IN JOIGNY

"AAHHH! *Le chien est dans le lit !*" We were harshly awakened by a chambermaid around noon. Even if in my slumberous state I hadn't detected a foreign accent, I knew a French person wouldn't have screamed at the discovery of a dog in the bed.

"*Calmez-vous*, Madame Rabaa. It's only a dog," a stern French voice replied. "Where is he supposed to sleep? On the floor?"

The door to my room slammed abruptly shut. "For example," I heard Madame Rabaa affirm from the other side. "Or better yet outside in the garden." There was no apology from either woman for barging in unannounced.

• • •

Calvados had done the trick of counteracting the red wine enough for me to be able to drive lucidly for several hours on mostly pitch-black roads, through miles of forest, but by the time we checked into our room at a small auberge in Montigny-sur-Loing, my head was pounding and my scalp tingling.

I'd had trouble getting to sleep; with JP's snoring amplified at the foot of my bed, I lay awake until dawn brought quiet to our room. JP doesn't move during the night—he sleeps like a log, albeit loudly—but at dawn he repositions himself from the floor to the pillow beside my head, and there he seems to know that he must not snore.

We didn't get reprimanded for a late checkout, but room service was out of the question. I was served a late breakfast on the terrace. The owner sat us at a table by the rushing Loing

River (in case JP wanted a drink), and we were served reluctantly by Madame Rabaa. As I plotted our course for the day and made a call from my portable phone to confirm dinner (that evening was to be our first five-star experience), she brought one item at a time over the course of about ten minutes—first bread, then butter, then coffee, then sugar, then milk.

JP ignored Madame Rabaa—he made himself invisible under the table, thereby, more importantly, making her invisible to him—and she in turn ignored me, until she couldn't help herself any longer. When she thought the owner was out of earshot, she almost hissed: "I hope you haven't left the dog in the room— I've got to go and sterilize it now."

JP popped his head out from under the table and she jumped. "God! He did that on purpose!"

I smiled. "Smart, isn't he?"

An English couple having lunch at the table next to me became very excited. "Look darling, it's a Dalmatian!"

JP stared at the woman, flapping his tail on the ground at her, flirting. Madame Rabaa rolled her eyes and said, "I thought you might have left him *in the bed*," so that they could hear.

The owner set down a bottle of water at the English table and, having overheard, said to me, "Don't pay any attention to her—she's jealous because she hasn't had anyone in her bed for ten years."

The English couple smiled, not understanding a word of what had been said, and Madame Rabaa left in a huff. "I'm the one who has to clean that room, not you," she added, under her breath.

"I can fix that anytime she wants," the owner added under hers.

• • •

We continued along the Loing River, stopping once so JP could harass some geese (who ended up harassing him). At La Genevraye we stumbled upon a thirteenth-century church in a field just off the main road. The stucco was falling off and old stone was peering through, and it looked unused and abandoned except for a cat who sat on a stone wall, teasing JP.

He was trying to determine whether he might be able to jump and reach the cat when there was a sudden screeching of tires on the dirt drive, followed by a horn. That caused the cat to jump off the wall—in turn sending JP in wild pursuit. The car, a beaten-up Fiat, belonged to Madame Rabaa.

"You forgot your portable phone at the table," she called out without shutting off the motor or exiting the car.

I walked over, smiling as best I could. "How did you know where to find us?" I asked.

"Lucky guess, judging from that map you had."

It was very kind of her to deliver the phone, and I told her that. She smiled, brightly for the first time, and JP came running back to jump up on her car and lick her face. "Gross!" she yelled, not meaning it, I realized. JP wouldn't stop and she finally had to give in and laugh, adding, "The only thing I hate worse than dogs is cats!" I pulled JP off her car. "Did you catch it at least?" she asked JP as she reversed. He glanced in the direction of the feline escape, then looked back at the now receding Fiat.

"*Bon voyage*," she waved without looking back.

The phone was blinking with a message—as it turned out, an urgent one from Madame Clix. The British owners of JP's betrothed had apparently miscalculated, and she was well into her heat. The "window of opportunity" would begin in a matter of days and would not last for long. Could we please hurry?

I clicked off the voice mail and looked over at JP, who was sniffing around the wall. I suddenly felt uneasy about him losing his virginity—he was a little boy to me. He turned to look at me, tilting his head, looking more like a puppy than ever, obviously wondering why I was staring at him. "*On y va*," I said. He joyfully ran to me, gave me a nuzzle, and then mounted the scooter, en route to manhood.

I consulted our map for a more direct course to Joigny. Following the Loing River as I'd planned would take longer, so we cut across the wooded countryside to the Lunain River. Then we traveled along rather uninteresting roads until we got to the Yonne River at Saint-Julien-du-Sault, where JP took a muddy dip before dinner.

Despite the shortcut, it was nearly nightfall when we crossed the bridge into Joigny, a medieval town with narrow cobbled streets, courtyards full of flowers, and timber-framed fifteenth- and sixteenth-century buildings and churches. We stopped at the gate of St. Jean, a preserved remnant of the original fortified city wall, and managed to cause a small commotion when JP got off the scooter and lifted his leg.

A couple of children sitting at a sidewalk café with their parents giggled and pointed at JP just as a busload of Japanese tourists disembarked. They began to point, too, and flock around us, wanting to take pictures of the Frenchman with his Vespa and his dog.

"Wait!" one of them called out in English. I waited for a second but as the camera flashed, JP, as always, turned away.

"Oh!" several people squealed. I could see one man in the rearview mirror entering the road, frantically snapping his camera as we accelerated in the direction of our reason for coming to Joigny.

La Côte Saint-Jacques is a highly rated restaurant for those in the know, but I hadn't expected a valet and a hostess to be standing outside the entrance upon our arrival. The mud had dried on JP, and he'd be brown until he shook it off; and I, windblown, in shorts and a T-shirt, contributed to the shabby sight. I tried to avoid eye contact with the welcome committee and sped past the restaurant until I could turn off the main road toward the river. I found a quiet spot along the bank of the Yonne where I attempted to make us presentable.

When even a stick tossed into the water didn't entice JP to rinse off (especially not when he knew it was dinnertime), I was forced to push him into the river. I then gave myself the best Evian bath I could. With the help of some hair gel, jeans, blue

Oxford shirt, and black jacket (my only "dress clothes"), I transformed myself into a (hopefully) suitable patron. I asked JP what he thought, but he turned away, very annoyed with me. As I matted down a final strand of windswept hair, satisfied, thinking we'd never be recognized as the peasant and mutt who'd just whizzed by, my phone rang.

"*Monsieur ? Ici le restaurant La Côte Saint-Jacques. Vous êtes perdus ?*" a concerned woman's voice asked.

"Ahm, no, not lost. We're almost there," I said.

After a short silence the woman said, "Oh, *bien sûr, aucun problème*, it's just that I thought I saw you drive by and I wanted to make sure you hadn't missed us."

So much for our discreet transformation. "*Merci beaucoup, Madame, à tout de suite*," I said. At least we wouldn't be turned away.

•   •   •

"That," said an elegant woman in her late sixties whom I took to be the wife of the renowned chef Jean-Michel Lorain, "is the most beautiful dog I have ever seen." JP waited until I had parked the scooter in front of the restaurant before shaking off the remaining river water, prancing up to Madame Lorain, allowing himself to be caressed, and entering through the main door. "*Ce n'est pas possible*," she added, laughing at his intelligence—or boldness, I wasn't sure which.

"Oh, it's true," I said. He was angry with me for cleaning him up for dinner, and he wouldn't be waiting for me. I got off the scooter and approached JP with his leash. He stepped aside.

"He's prettier without it anyway," the woman said, smiling. She led us to an elevator, which took us to an underground tunnel that led to an empty cavelike lounge. She then took my order for an aperitif. So that was it: We'd be hidden, dining underground, no matter how beautiful she thought JP was. Before she retreated she said, "A Madame Clix telephoned for you. She said it's extremely urgent that you call her."

·   ·   ·

"Oh I've been sick, *tout à fait malade*, with worry! Didn't you receive my message this morning?" was how Madame Clix answered her phone, without so much as a hello.

"Sorry, we've been on the road all day—but I did get your message and we'll hurry," I said.

"*Monsieur ?*" A young waiter arrived with my aperitif and some *accompagnements*.

"*Un instant, s'il vous plaît*," I said into the phone, and then set it down, as the waiter placed several small plates strategically around the coffee table. He explained the Iranian caviar toasts, poached quail eggs, and prosciutto with basil.

"Are you still there?" Madame Clix spoke so loudly that the waiter heard.

"*Excusez-moi, Monsieur*," he said, and stepped back several yards from the table, one hand still holding the tray with the makings for my gin and tonic, his other hand respectfully by his side, waiting until I dealt with the woman on the phone. A second waiter arrived with another tray. As he approached, the first waiter motioned for him to stop. They both waited.

"Yes, I'm still here . . . I'm having dinner," I said.

"You *are* the one who phoned me, after all. I mean, if you were dining—" She went on to explain that Flirt would be arriving sooner than expected, and that the dogs would need some time to get to know one other before *l'acte d'amour* so that the right hormones and odors would be excreted. Otherwise the puppies might not be *normaux*.

When she stopped to catch her breath, I asked Madame Clix how she knew where to find me.

"It wasn't easy!" she said dramatically, suspiciously, as if I had intentionally kept my daily whereabouts a secret. "Our friend Laurent told me you'd planned a gastronomic journey and I called all the Michelin star restaurants until I found you. I'm sure they think I'm insane, *complètement folle !*" In fact, Laurent had told me exactly that—he had spent a summer working for her as part of a work-study program for students of veterinary medicine.

"Please make certain you've got a nice, soft towel on that *moto* for JP to sit on. We don't want his *zizis* bouncing around and getting injured. And you won't drive *too* fast, will you," she said, and hung up.

"Sorry," I said to the waiters.

"*C'est nous.* It is we who are sorry," said the first waiter as he set down a tall glass and, using tongs, placed four perfectly round ice cubes, one by one, into it. He dispensed the gin from a decanter, filling the glass halfway, and then began to pour a small amount of Schweppes very slowly. With another set of tongs he positioned a wedge of lemon on the rim of the glass.

The other waiter set a silver bowl filled with ice cubes on the floor by JP and poured a bottle of Vittel into it. It made a crackly noise that piqued JP's interest. Both waiters smiled for the first time, dropping their formality. "*Il est magnifique, votre chien,*" they said in unison.

"Truly," the maître d'hôtel said as he approached. "*Monsieur, soyez les bienvenus,*" he continued, with an exaggerated smile. "A bit of reading material, perhaps." He handed me the menu and set the wine list on the table. "It has just been printed so there are no substitutions or additions this evening." JP looked at him expectantly, and he reached down and caressed him.

I glanced only quickly at the menu (mainly just to see the price of the *prix fixe* menus) and set the voluminous thing down. There was too much to choose from, and in restaurants like this, because I have a really hard time making up my mind and hate the idea of missing out on anything, I almost always order the *menu dégustation* of samplers. At this particular restaurant it was called the *menu surprise* of unspecified market-fresh ingredients.

I tried to win back JP's affections with a quail egg. He refused, still pouting. I sat back and looked around at the subterranean room—with Roman sculptures against limestone walls, and handwoven tapestries covering the floors. I was happy we were dining alone like this, even if we had been exiled, isolated from the more civilized patrons. Paris, only one hundred miles away, seemed like a faraway place. And so did *le domaine Clix*. I thought about my first visit to *le domaine*, one of the more remarkable and intimidating experiences I'd had in my life.

•   •   •

Madame Clix had told me that I was to wait outside the gate to her property until she came for me—the visit would be timed so that the puppies could nurse in peace. Apparently my scent could upset the mother and her flow of milk. One side of the wrought-iron gate swung on weathered stone columns, open, one of its hinges broken; the other was closed, overgrown with ivy. Beyond the gate was a limestone fountain, stagnant and green with algae, but rich underneath with intricate carvings. The only sound was an occasional drip from one of its spouts.

After I'd been there for about half an hour, a distinguished, ageless voice, from somewhere I couldn't quite place, said: "All right, come see the tree, then." From around the side of the manor house stepped a woman who appeared tall, but as she came closer was revealed to be of less-than-average height—but of extraordinary presence. She was a combination of innate elegance and country neglect: Jet-black hair overflowed from underneath her tight-fitting knit cap as if she'd been through a storm, but none of the probably sixty-year-old strands was gray. She wore a tight, black silk skirt, an oversized scarf was more or less draped over her, and her finely lined face was tan and free of any makeup.

"It's over here." She picked up an armful of ivy and walked back the way she'd come. "And if you brought as much as you can carry with you, I wouldn't object." She led me to a smoking bonfire of ivy and branches.

There was a patio covered by a trellis of bougainvillea and grapevines extending from the back of the house until it merged into lavender shrubs, ivy, and wildflowers. Everything seemed to ramble on for a hilly, rolling acre all the way to a rippling stream. One side of the patio was protected by a stone wall that had been built into the side of a small hill, and on that wall was *the tree*: a glass-encased charcoal rendering of a family tree of various Dalmatians, with sketches of each dog, his or her name, and dates of birth and death. It represented the Dalmatians *le domaine* had raised since 1710.

Sketches of two of the oldest dogs had black spots, faded with age, but all of the others were a distinct liver brown. At the yellowed base of the tree were the Adam and Eve of the line of the du Bois-de-Tanagra family, the King and Queen Jean-François (liver) and Marguerite (black). At the top of the ever-growing tree were eleven bare branches recently penciled in.

Madame Clix nodded to it, an indication that I should inspect it, and then walked toward the barn. "Not a crossed cousin, aunt, uncle, or grandparent . . . and not a drop of red blood," she threw back with a slight tilt of her head. Madame Clix's blood was no doubt blue as well.

The outside of the barn was a weathered gray, with two small, shiny windows framed by large shutters of faded blue on either side of tall wooden doors. The interior was more like the living room of a Parisian loft than the inside of a barn, complete with sofas, lamps, and other accoutrements. At one side of the "room," on a very comfortable-looking *chaise longue*, was an elegant *dalmatienne* (very evidently a female), looking as if she were made of porcelain—pointedly paying us no notice.

Across from her, in a large crib most definitely built for human occupancy, was another female, along with half a dozen infants, all but one clinging to their mother's udder competing for nipples. I walked up to the crib and poked my fingers through. The puppies waddled over to me competitively, except for the one who dozed contentedly in a corner: He had a pink-and-brown nose, mostly dark brown ears, a shiny white coat with a few scattered spots poking through, and rings of brown circling his eyes. He opened one slowly and stretched, and then, taking advantage of the absence of his siblings, went straight to a nipple and drank unhindered while the others were busy suckling my fingers. I knew that sly little monster was for me.

"Puppies always choose their people, not the other way around." Madame Clix must have noticed my charmed expression.

"Do you think that one likes me?" I asked stupidly, as he was totaling ignoring me.

"It doesn't look like it." She shrugged. "But then he hasn't really bonded with anyone."

I was surprised at how sure I was about this puppy. "I think I'll take him," I said, stroking his fur.

Madame Clix corrected me: "What you'll do, *jeune homme,*

since you *think* you really want him, is come back in a couple of weeks when the puppy's sight is better, and then we'll see if he has reconsidered. For the moment we need to see if his *maman* likes the scent of you."

•   •   •

"Asleep already?" Monsieur Lorain himself said to JP, jolting me back to the present and instantly waking JP. "I was told I had to come down to see this *merveille de création.*" Well aware that he was being referred to, JP stood up and waited to see what his prize might be for being such a marvel. He waited patiently while the chef made an effort to focus on me. "*Monsieur,*" he said, smiling. "Have you found something that tempts your palate?"

I opened the menu and pointed to the *menu surprise.*

"*Parfait,*" he said. "Perfect. Is there any ingredient you don't care for?"

I told him that I liked everything except onions. "*Parfait,*" he said. "Gilbert will see you about the wine."

The chef's smile widened noticeably as he turned back to JP. "And the little man? What would he like?" JP's stomach had been rumbling loudly since we arrived. "Something isn't sitting well with him, I suspect," the chef said, genuinely concerned.

I explained about the liver overdose, and, mostly to be polite, suggested something bland like egg whites. JP groaned.

Getting warm receptions and good tables at canine-friendly restaurants was one thing, but having your dog's order taken by a five-star chef who probably wasn't in the habit of taking human orders was treatment I don't think even JP could take for granted: As a token of gratitude for the *attention particulière*, he made a rather conspicuous display of rolling over and presenting his ailing belly to the chef.

"Nonsense," the chef protested, taking the hint and scratching JP's underside. "As with any kind of *excès*, the only cure is more of the same, lest the *malade* suffer from withdrawal, which is worse than anything." He then made a note to himself: "*Très bien*, one *menu surprise* for *Monsieur*, and a platter of *foie gras* and *pâté* for *Monsieur*." He smiled at us, individually. "I imagine you'll share your bread with him," he said to me. "Of course we normally serve the *foie gras* with brioches, but perhaps a rice *accompagnement* would be best for him. *Bon appétit, Messieurs*," he said, and winked at JP.

Gilbert, sporting an enormous medallion on a chain around his neck, recognition for being a world-class sommelier, also had a surprise suggestion. Thankfully he didn't propose that I share it with JP, since his decided preference for the wine that could be best *marié* with my dinner was a Blagny costing two hundred euros (*roughly two hundred dollars*, I thought with panic) and double the cost of the food. Of course he also suggested a few other possibilities, but with such a lack of enthusiasm that I didn't consider them.

"If you would like to pass to the dining room," he said, delighted with my choice, when I didn't object.

My paranoia had been unfounded, I realized, as Gilbert led us from the *salon apéritif* to the real dining room upstairs, where we were seated at one of the best tables, in the corner, overlooking the lit gardens. JP's silver bowl with Vittel and fresh ice soon followed.

Here we were served the longest, most relaxing, and most delicious meal I have ever eaten. It was only after eight courses of dishes such as a gratin of oysters, *tartare* of scallops, truffled beef, and literally dozens of cheeses (of which JP also partook after his liver and rice dishes), as I was curing my previous night's *excès* of Calvados with a Bas Armagnac, this time in an upstairs lounge, that I realized how exhausted I was—and that we hadn't booked a room anywhere.

Sobered, I asked for the check. *"Mais Monsieur,"* the waiter said. "Of course you can take care of that when you check out in the morning. I'll bring your key—it's to one of our loveliest rooms overlooking the Yonne."

"I won't be spending the night," I said. There was no way I could drop another several hundred euros on a riverfront room at this Relais & Châteaux establishment.

The waiter looked at me confusedly and said, *"Pardonnez-moi."* He would return, I thought, with the check.

He returned instead with a key and the hostess. "Did the *madame* who telephoned not arrange this with you?" she asked. At my perplexed look she continued. "I'm terribly embarrassed, but Madame Clix said that you were to enjoy dinner and a good night's sleep with us . . . entirely courtesy of her." Before I could translate my astonishment into words, she added: "And under no circumstances were we to allow you to object."

ESCAPE FROM CHARITÉ

JP SHIFTED AND leaned into my right thigh when we were at the light, in the direction of a flirtatious chocolate Labrador sunbathing by an empty bench. She was staring at JP, and I could feel his tail trying to wag between my shins—he was feeling frisky, his stomach ailment apparently cured by the infusion of liver. We'd gotten an early start, and with my neck and back aches having been soothed by an incredible sleep on a firm king-sized mattress, I was intent on putting some serious miles behind us before we stopped for a late lunch—the *pique-nique surprise* the restaurant had prepared and packed for us. I turned left, away from the Labrador, in the direction of the banks of the Loire toward Nevers, I felt JP's diaphragm lift and sink as he sighed deeply against my knee. He contorted his neck to be able to watch the object of his affection for as long as he could.

A few miles later, as the road narrowed, a *contrôle* was being conducted by several gendarmes. I had already noticed that these random inspections usually occur in the most unlikely and remote places where there were the fewest motorists. A uniformed teenager signaled to me with a swoop of his arm and an index finger. I pulled over to the side of the road, and JP stepped off before I could stop him.

"Eh eh eh! *Sa laisse !* His leash! This is a thoroughfare, not a park!" the young man shouted.

It was a one-lane, paved trail, but I summoned JP: "*D'accord*—JP, *viens ici.*" JP humbly obeyed and returned to sit by the scooter.

An older gendarme nodded to the younger as if giving him

permission to question me. The gendarme-in-training strutted over, unhurried, intent on finding me guilty of something. *"Vos papiers, s'il vous plaît."* He pronounced the *vos papiers* in a very mature, official-sounding tone, but the *please* part was barely audible. He also seemed to be addressing JP, with whom he was making direct eye contact, and so I reached for JP's French passport, which I kept in my zippered jacket pocket next to mine.

A similar tactic had once been successful with a Parisian policeman who let me go without a ticket after JP and I had used a sidewalk to pass a car. (*When in Paris do as the Parisians*, I'd figured.) Parisian gendarmes have more important things to do than arrest weaving two-wheelers, and earning a smile is so rare for them that they're more than amenable to let a cheery offender go. Motorists view being pulled over as extremely ill-mannered treatment—*évidemment* if they weren't in a hurry for some very good reason they wouldn't have been speeding—and if they do bother to roll down their windows for such an imposition it's not to exchange pleasantries but rather to argue their cases aggressively, often in advance of the accusation.

Provincial gendarmes, as I was about to learn, have more time than they know what to do with, and get their fill of laughs among themselves all day long; they don't expect funny business from a potential offender.

"What's this?" he asked, still glaring at JP. I noticed that his face still had peach fuzz.

"His papers," I smiled.

"*Your* papers, Monsieur." He frowned. "Driver's license and *carte grise* for the scooter, *s'il vous plaît.*" This time the *please* part was overly emphasized. I handed him the papers he wanted.

"What's this?" he asked again.

"It's my driver's license."

"From where?"

"New York," I pointed out, indicating with my finger the name of the state in large letters at the top of the card.

"What are you doing here?" he demanded, as if he'd never before encountered a foreigner.

"I'm a student," I said, stretching the truth.

"At what school?"

"La Sorbonne. The term has just ended," I admitted.

"La Sorbonne is in Paris. I asked what you were doing *here,* not in Paris," he said.

"I'm on vacation" seemed an easier answer than "I'm going to breed my dog," so I tried it. He wasn't impressed.

"What's this?" he asked yet again, this time questioning the photocopy of my gray card, the French moniker for a vehicle registration card.

"It's my *carte grise.*"

He shook his head. "No, it isn't. The original is in Paris where you're a student, *j'imagine ?*"

I nodded.

He shook his head. "What's in that?" he asked, pointing to the lunch basket from La Côte Saint-Jacques that I had secured to the seat behind me with rubber straps.

"Lunch," I said, motioning for him to verify. He in turn nodded his head at it, indicating that I should open it.

The older gendarme walked over. "*Monsieur*," he greeted me with a bit more civility. "Is there a problem, Ludo?" he asked.

Ludo exhaled and shook his head dramatically. "*Ooh, là.* Is there ever. A photocopied registration. Foreign license. And a dog." He pronounced the word *photocopy* as if it were a forgery and *dog* as if it were contraband.

"La Côte Saint-Jacques. *Pas mal*, not bad," said the older gendarme, noticing the embossed linen napkin the restaurant had placed on top of the food.

Ludo lifted the napkin to peek underneath, confirming the contents. "Yes, not bad at all for a student," he said suspiciously and walked to a small blue gendarme's car.

"Cute dog. Is he friendly?" the older gendarme asked me.

I nodded.

"He's new on the job."

I tried to smile. "What's he doing?" I asked.

"Running a check on your papers. Making sure you're not wanted by Interpol or something."

"No one's picking up at the gendarmerie," Ludo complained as if to say, *Now look at the trouble you've caused.*

The older gendarme shrugged. I took the shrug to mean that we'd be allowed to go.

Ludo had another idea. "I'll have to ask you to follow me on your scooter. Hold on to these," he said, handing me the papers.

"Just in case." I suppose that meant in case real policemen pulled me over on the way.

The older gendarme smiled fraternally at JP and me both, and then shrugged, as if we, too, should find the apprenticeship as charming as he seemed to. "I've got a pointer. Great dog," he said.

·   ·   ·

We were greeted warmly by a group of gendarmes playing *boules* in the courtyard of the gendarmerie of La Charité-sur-Loire. The sight of JP arriving *en scooter* was enough for them to pause the game.

"*Hé*, look at that!" one of them said as we pulled up on the scooter.

"How do you get him to sit still on that? I've never seen anything like that before," said another, kneeling down to greet JP, who was already entering the game and clumsily displacing a few of the balls.

"Neither have I," said Ludo.

Ludo's mentor explained to the group that Ludo wasn't convinced it was legal. "He tried to radio you but no one picked up."

The *boules*-playing men looked at one another. "No one's inside?" asked one with mock surprise.

"I thought Jérôme was," said another.

"I'm right here, beating the pants off you!" said Jérôme. He smiled at me. "Well if no one's ever seen it before, chances are no one has ever thought of a law against it. *Non ?*" He nudged my shoulder. "You don't agree?"

I said, "Oh, I definitely agree." They laughed heartily—all except Ludo, who went inside.

"He's doing this job for the summer as part of his military service," Jérôme shrugged. "He's going to be a lawyer like his father." I gathered from his tone that Ludo's father was an important but disliked man.

•   •   •

JP's sad eyes penetrated mine. The day had gotten hotter as the afternoon wore on. I looked into the office window of the gendarmerie from the parking lot where we had been "impounded" for more than three hours while Ludo researched the legality of dogs on scooters. During this time Jérôme had gone home, after apologizing to us and assuring me that nothing would come of any of this nonsense.

JP mounted the scooter, panting. I could feel his thought: *Why are we sitting here?*

And I was thinking: *Why didn't I turn left and let JP play with the Labrador?*

The lot was otherwise empty and I took out JP's rubber ball to see if he might be interested in a game of catch, but he sat even more upright, unwavering in his determination not to dismount . . . and that we be on our way.

Let's go, he whimpered. It was tempting: There was enough

room for a scooter to squeeze past the barrier, and I had all my papers. I was infused with that naive invincibility one sometimes feels in a foreign place, where ignorance of the law *is* an excuse. I slid up the kickstand and rolled JP past the barrier. My chest was pounding. I didn't dare look again in the direction of the office, but focused instead on the open road beckoning us. I pushed the scooter harder, faster, and when I was sure we were safely enough away, started the motor and revved it.

JP's mouth was hanging open, smiling, and I laughed when we passed the sign reading, THANK YOU FOR VISITING LA CHARITÉ. I accelerated, and flew until my heart stopped racing. As the countryside replaced villages, bright ribbons of red and yellow began to form ahead of us, glimmering in the sunlight on the horizon. I sped up. With the warm wind in my hair (my helmet was strapped to my arm, which definitely was a crime), I felt a proud exhilaration. Being pursued for no real crime seemed unlikely, and getting caught seemed like an impossibility; but even if we were to end up behind bars, it would have been worth it for this moment of thrill. As if sensing this, JP turned his muzzle up and out to let the full force of the air into his mouth, sucking it in. I revved the engine as high as it would go.

The red and yellow ribbons were fantastic fields of wild poppies, on either side of the road, for as far as the eye could see. The terrain was slightly hilly and rolling, and the flowers looked like velvet cushions. I imagined that if we leapt into them we'd sink into their softness and bounce off unharmed. I slowed down to be able to see the individual plants, so much did the fields look like fabric.

As we coasted along at a more reasonable speed, worries began to creep upon me. By escaping, the police would think I had something to hide, and my paranoia of being spotted increased as we passed a few other cars and they waved at JP. Of course we could sneak out—but we'd always be conspicuous. By now they had surely discovered that we were missing; other districts would be notified. JP, too, became acutely aware of our surroundings, paying careful attention to the fields, seeing and smelling things like rabbits and farmers.

I thought I'd seen water glistening through a break in the poppies. I applied the brakes and turned sharply—a little too sharply—and lost control in the gravelly shoulder of the road. There was no chance of avoiding a spill and I shouted to JP: "Jump!"

Amazingly, we both jumped without hesitation at the exact same moment. I landed on my side in a pile of soft dirt, JP on his four feet, skidding. The scooter spun around on its side like a top, over and over, in the middle of the road, its engine screeching and smoking.

JP rushed over to me, sniffed my neck, and, determining that I was unharmed, licked my face and bounded off really wanting this to be a game. When my head and the scooter had stopped spinning, I squatted down and put the motor out of its misery. As the desperation of the situation was about to hit me, JP returned to lick my face repeatedly, loving me, with or without wheels. I let him lick and lick and lick while I thought about what to do.

All of a sudden JP had had enough, and he bolted to the side of the road. He had set the pace, and I hoisted the scooter and pushed it to the side of the road. No sooner had I done so than I heard the faint sound of a siren, and once again my heart started racing. JP jumped into the poppies and I followed him, pushing the scooter as hard and fast as I could into the moist soil of the field, where I let it fall. I looked back to catch a glimpse of the police car approaching. JP stopped. His white coat stood out against the bright red and I shouted to him: "Down!" He was on the ground, prone, in an instant. I laid the scooter down flat, ran to JP, and lay down with him. The car sped past us, siren blaring.

I detached the lunch basket and saddle box, uprooted as many poppy plants as I could, and camouflaged the scooter. JP stretched, already eager for the next adventure, and walked toward the water. I gathered our things and caught up with him. After about twenty yards the poppy field began to slope down and we found ourselves entering a valley with a calm, wide river carving its way through it. JP ran down to the river and jumped in. I ran after him, losing my clothes piece by piece along the way. I waded in. The pebbly bottom was soft and the water was warm and clear.

JP swam blissfully in circles, cleansing himself of the dirt from the fall and the stress of the day. When I was up to my neck, JP dog-paddled toward me; I swam in the opposite direction to avoid his scratching claws. He pursued me, both of us paddling as fast as we could, JP faster. Luckily for my back, a stick had dared to float past JP and he preoccupied himself with that while I put some distance between us until we were both out of breath.

Back on the shore, the setting sun cast a crimson reflection onto the water. JP gave me a look to let me know it was that time of day, no matter how far from a restaurant we might be. I opened our picnic lunch that was about to become our dinner: liver and rice for JP; lamb, roasted garlic and grilled vegetable sandwich, Brie-de-Meaux cheese, fresh fruit, and a half bottle of another nice Blagny (complete with bottle opener and a wineglass that had somehow survived the spill) for me. The real surprise part of the *pique-nique* was a soft terry-cloth blanket for us to eat it on—and, as it turned out, to sleep on, under a black sky of dancing stars.

SPELLS ON THE
RIVER ALLIER

JP HAD AWAKENED me several times during the night—barking, warding off unseen menaces, his rarely seen canine instincts taking over—but I had otherwise slept soundly enough on our bed of terry-cloth and pebbles. And aside from one or two nagging mosquito bites, I felt refreshed and surprisingly undaunted by the tasks that lay ahead, including that of fixing or replacing the scooter. My first early-morning concern was how to feed my caffeine addiction.

When JP saw that I was awake at the crack of dawn and able to alert myself to any danger, he stretched and yawned loudly (he hadn't slept quite as well and he wanted me to know) and wandered off to find a place for his ablutions. I put some of the previous night's liver and rice into his bowl for when he returned, found some soap and shampoo, stripped off my wrinkled clothes, and stepped into the river, where I lathered myself up.

I saw that JP had something in his mouth as he came toward me, and could tell by the excitedly guilty wag of his tail that it wasn't just a stick. He was a puppy the last time he'd done the very doglike thing of demolishing and digesting a steak bone someone had given him. We'd spent that night in the twenty-four-hour veterinary emergency room in Paris, and JP hadn't touched another bone since that incident.

"What have you got there, JP?" I thought it might be the bone of a wild animal carcass. I stood up from the water, revealing most of my naked body, when I noticed that JP wasn't alone—he was followed by four figures dressed in white robes. I knelt down in the water.

"Nothing I haven't seen before," said a woman's voice. She came up behind JP and scratched his back. "She's a beauty, this one," the woman said.

JP moved away from her and dropped the thick piece of rope that had served as a tie for the woman's robe.

"He," I said. I myself sometimes unconsciously assign JP's gender to other dogs I encounter.

"Of course he is," the woman said, picking up the rope and teasing JP with it. "I've got a Labrador at home who would love to tug his *corde*." JP looked at me for a sign of approval and then gave in to her.

The other people were now talking quietly among themselves, and thankfully facing the other way while I remained as hidden as I could. The woman, however, walked to the edge of the water and looked directly at me. She leaned down, put her hand in the water, and splashed some onto her face.

Close up, I could see that she was about thirty, attractive, and more or less normal looking if you forgot the attire. "Are you thirsty?" she asked.

I was, actually, and I nodded. "How long have you been in the water?" she asked.

"I don't know, ten minutes, maybe."

"That's all it takes. There are lots of minerals and traces of salt in the Allier—it feeds from the same underground sources as Vichy. That's why we're here," she said. "Great for the soul, but it dehydrates the body. You might want to get out." She considerately turned her back to me and said lightheartedly to her friends, "Don't look, *les filles*, he's not comfortable in his skin," and then to me, "What are you, anyway, English?" As if that would explain being modest.

I got out of the water and strode quickly toward my clothes. "American," I said. This was becoming routine. There was gasping in unison and the heads of three women and one man turned toward me as I pulled my jeans up my wet legs, struggling where they were sticking at the knees. When I'd gotten them zipped, the woman who found me uncomfortable in my skin held out an unlabeled bottle of water.

"*Voilà*," she said. She looked down at JP, who had settled down beside me. "*Zhay-pay* ? Is that what I heard you call him?" She studied him for a few long seconds and then looked deeply into my eyes. "Whoa," she said, "you're powerful, you two." There was another collective gasp.

I poured some water into my hand and held it out to JP. I thought I'd better have him sniff it—just in case. JP lapped it up and then charged playfully at the woman. I felt safe taking a swig.

"That's it," she said to JP, "focus on Ghislaine," apparently meaning herself. "So the Allier has summoned you as well," she said to me.

"Yes, it's a pretty river," I said, pulling a T-shirt over my head. There were nods and sighs of agreement.

"Hmmph," Ghislaine said, "Not particularly, not as far as French waters go." More sighs of agreement; it was obvious that whoever, whatever they were, Ghislaine was the group leader. "Are you headed upstream or downstream?" she asked.

"I'm traveling by scooter," I said. "Or at least I was."

The group laughed. "Are you heading to the north of France or the south," she clarified.

"South," I said. Ghislaine nodded reflectively. "Are you part of a church?" I asked, curious, and as a way to fill the heavy silence that had enveloped us.

This question was met with more silence and more intense scrutiny until Ghislaine said, "You're not a wizard."

"No." I smiled, thinking it was just another French joke I didn't get. "Are you witches?" I joked back. I picked up our blanket and shook off the sand.

"We most certainly are," said the one man, indignantly, not thrilled that they'd seriously taken me for one.

"Oh, he is a *sorcier*, all right, Patrick," Ghislaine said. "He just doesn't know it yet." Patrick looked doubtful. "Remember when you came to me for your first reading? You had no idea you had power." This seemed to ring true with Patrick, and he shrugged.

Ghislaine stroked JP, who had settled in beside her. "Now, is that dog a *conducteur* or what?" she asked her friends. They sighed in agreement. "Have you ever known a *conducteur*, a dog *or* a cat medium, to share the same space with a powerless man?"

"*Non*," the group concurred, again in unison.

"*Voilà*," she said, confirming that I must possess power I didn't know about.

"Yes, that's JP—with me through thick or thin." I didn't know what else to say, but I didn't like that JP liked Ghislaine so much.

"You know, he'd be very useful for some spells," she said. I hoped she didn't mean as an animal sacrifice, but in any case I figured that now was as good a time as any to take my leave in search of some coffee.

"Fancy a coffee?" Ghislaine asked.

"Great idea," someone else answered. Suddenly the ambience changed and they seemed like normal people.

• • •

"Animals are in direct contact with God, unlike us. We humans have to set up channels. Actually, you Americans are wonderful with that," Patrick said, happy that I liked coffee as strong as he did.

They had come prepared: sterno stove, cookware, freshly ground coffee, and a French press. JP had sniffed all the paraphernalia and wagged approvingly before I indulged myself. Their campsite was about a hundred yards from mine, and Ghislaine swore that JP had visited them several times during the night—which I found difficult to believe.

"That's why we were so impressed—we thought you'd come here all the way from America to practice. Here, we've either got the gift or not, depending on whether it was in the blood of our ancestors. We've got some useful spells passed down from the Knights of Templar and some North African rituals, but you people across the Atlantic have the channeling thing down to a science."

I sipped, smiled, and said "Em" as politely as I could muster.

"You don't believe in it, but you're someone who could hear your heart if you'd only take the time to stop and listen. Right there is magic," Ghislaine said. "And I can tell you something else. It is no accident that you stumbled upon us." Suddenly she burst out in a contagious giggle that got me laughing, too—and JP wagging delightedly. "Or I should say it was an accident that got you here!"

They had already found my story of wiping out very funny, and, like all the French country folk I'd encountered thus far, fateful. I didn't feel like laughing at the play on words; my scooter was a serious problem.

Ghislaine picked up on my change of mood. "You may follow your heart and that takes you in the right direction, but accidents happen when you're on the wrong path getting there," she said metaphorically. "And you know perfectly well what I mean, don't you?" She looked deeply into my eyes, sending a chill up my spine. I stood up and nodded.

"Don't go rushing off—that won't help you. You need to do the opposite: Find some calm, the calm that's in there," Ghislaine said, pointing to my heart. "I'll make a deal with you. You spend a couple of hours with us, and we'll cast a spell on you that will get you safely and quickly to the south—and even more than that, you'll be *charmé* : Everything you encounter will be wonderful, and you'll attract only good things," she proposed. "Guaranteed." I looked at my watch, about to graciously refuse. "And Patrick will repair your scooter. He is a mechanic by trade, after all. As long as it's not smashed up—he's useless with body work." She laughed.

"So what do I have to do?" I asked. I couldn't refuse a deal like that; anyway, the idea of white magic intrigued me.

"Not a thing," she said. "Just let us use your spotted medium there for a spell or two—all he has to do is sit still."

If he will sit still, I thought but didn't say.

"Oh, he'll sit still," Ghislaine said. "He's a natural."

. . .

While Ghislaine prepared for the ceremony, Monique, a small, heavyset, wrinkled woman of about fifty, assured me that it would be quick and painless. She went on to tell me about her background and that of the group. She was traveling with her ex-daughter-in-law, Sandrine. "My scoundrel of a son ran off to Spain with a Gypsy," she said. That was okay, though, since Sandrine was her true "soul-daughter," and had been her mother in another life.

All four of the witches lived in a small village in the Pyrénées, along with other witches who were on their own pilgrimages in France and beyond. All but Monique, a native of the village, had moved from various places across the country to live with others like themselves, in a colony where they could hone their craft. Ghislaine, Monique, and Patrick had been making the pilgrimage every summer to Lourdes, across the center of France and upward to Paris. They collected vials of waters that had been touched (and therefore blessed) by the Knights of Templar, and the red petals of poppy plants, which were a powerful ingredient of the red ink used to write incantations.

Although Monique's great, great, great, great grandfather had been the wizard of the count who once inhabited the derelict château in their village, Ghislaine's ancestral connection to magic came from both sides of her family. It was therefore deeper, and she had become the leader of the coven.

Monique's magic didn't have a price; she offered it to people free of charge, even to her wealthy employers (to earn a living she had been cleaning the vacation homes of the Germans, British, and Parisians who had been moving en masse to the southwest of France for years), many of whom had apparently grown so dependent on her that they hardly made a move, never so much as bought a stock, without calling her first. They phoned her day and night (indeed, her mobile phone had rung several times during our conversation), but they did of course shower her with gifts, most of which she gave to her daughter-in-law. She told me how she now only executed *des sorts blancs*, white spells, which brought about exclusively good fortune. She had once cast a *sort noir*, a black magic spell, on the unfaithful husband of a vengeful Parisian woman, and it had worked; the husband was faithful for a few months, but then he became so unhappy without his mistress that he ended up committing suicide.

I admitted that I'd seen a psychic or two, and that I had felt it my destiny to come to France. She told me I had certainly lived in France in another life, but was still searching for my home—that I hadn't found it in Paris. Monique the cleaning woman/fortune-teller was proud of what she was, convinced of who she was, sure of her past, present, and future, and what that stood for, sure of where she belonged. She made me feel as if I wasn't sure about anything.

"You'll be home soon," she said, as certain about her prediction as she was about herself.

·   ·   ·

Not only did JP sit still, but he actually slept through the spells, which involved the burning of incense, splashing water from the Allier over everyone including him, and reciting simple incantations in the form of a prayer to God. It was difficult to grasp the specifics of what they were doing, but there was nothing malevolent about any of their words. And the mere fact that JP lay in the center of the circle as a channel was apparently sufficient to magnify the power of the white magic. They began by huddling around JP and praying in whispers (during which time I was asked to step away), and then Ghislaine cast the first three spells. After each of her passionately recited incantations, a parchment was passed around from witch to witch; they wrote French, Hebrew, and Arabic words on it with poppy ink. This, I was told, would "seal" the spell and should be carried by the charmed person to ensure its success.

Ghislaine asked Monique to cast the final spell. Monique seemed surprised and flattered and I gathered that this had not been part of the plan. The spells thus far were to benefit friends or family not present, but Monique's was the most touching in its sincerity and simplicity, I thought. The intended person—I took this to be her son—was first and foremost to "find his way home." Until then he was to be blessed with a "cloud" of good fortune that would cover and protect him from evil. Nothing could penetrate it except a light that would bestow the clarity of wisdom upon him so that he would find his way to the love of the soul and the treasures of the world (in that order, she emphasized) that he was destined to have. When she was finished, JP woke and stretched, but Ghislaine asked him to sit while the parchment was written. He did.

Monique wrote on the parchment first, and then dusted it with incense ash. After the others had written their part, Patrick folded it over and over into a small square of about half an inch, and placed it in my hand, covering it with his own. "I think your journey should be a safe one from this point on," he said. "Now let's have a look at that scooter."

CAUTION TO THE
WIND OF GANNAT

"Is everything all right? *Vous n'avez rien ?*" Madame Clix cried into the phone. No sooner had I pulled into a gas station on the outskirts of Varennes-sur-Allier to refuel than my cell phone went off. "I've been phoning all morning! I was afraid you'd been in an accident. I had a terrible dream that you two had fallen."

Monique's daughter-in-law had read my cards while Patrick repaired the scooter. She reported that I was *englouti*, engulfed by the powerful energy of a woman who meant well but was very demanding. A heartbroken but strong woman who was very intuitive—my mother in this life, or a previous one, and someone I should not disappoint. Sandrine had also pointed out that although I would be protected by their magic, I must be very cognizant of the choices I made in this lifetime because of the karmic debts they would incur.

"I'm really sorry," I said into the phone with as much sincerity as I could muster. "I'm trying to get there as fast as I can, that's all."

Short of breath, Madame said, "*Ah bon. C'est gentil.* But how long could a simple phone call take?"

Before hanging up I assured Madame that I would be there within two days, wondering how in the world I'd be able to pull it off. Luckily the only damage to the scooter had been the motor bracket—which Patrick had remounted—but even at maximum speed, on these small back roads we had about twenty hours of driving ahead of us.

As I pumped the gas, JP went to visit with the attendant. He was leaning against a wall on which was painted a giant map of the region. The man gave JP an obligatory pat, nothing more, and JP sat down beside him, all the while intently observing me, and me observing him, a game we liked to play. My eyes kept wandering to the map above his head, which was much more detailed than any of ours.

When I had finished pumping, I traced my finger along a small white road that ran alongside the Sioule River and the N9, the more direct but also more traveled *route nationale* we'd tried to avoid.

"You could probably follow that path with a scooter," the attendant said. "A car couldn't, though." I paid him, expecting him to at least comment on my journeying with a dog. But all he said was, "With *la grève*, the strike, the N-Nine will be impassable anyway."

The landscape along the banks of the Sioule was probably the most beautiful we'd seen so far. The entire region west of Vichy was picturesque, but the rolling geography on this particular route, with its forests, high plains, and extinct volcanoes at almost every vantage point was truly breathtaking. I couldn't help but stop to water JP every couple of miles just to be able to absorb our surroundings.

•   •   •

As we got farther downstream, we discovered that the *grève* this time (I'd already lived through a dozen or so major strikes in my four years in France) was launched by truckers protesting unfair wages. They blocked access to train stations, *autoroutes*, and any other means of transporting goods. As a result, even though the river road was direct, we were forced to stop at every point where it met a village. There it would be blocked by cars whose only alternate route to or from the north and south was the back roads. The cars were moving at a snail's pace in either direction, packed so closely together that at every crossroad JP and I had to stop and walk the scooter through the narrow spaces between bumpers that the occasional driver was kind enough to leave us.

At the village of Saint-Germain-de-Salles, JP had finally had enough of the stop-and-go driving; he stepped off the scooter. As usual, his timing was on the nose: Our gas supply was nearly depleted and it was almost one-forty-five, our last chance for a mid-day meal (while lunches can sometimes last until early evening, they can rarely be commenced after two in any region of France, at any restaurant). As usual, I would have to resort to something unconventional.

I coasted into the tiny village with JP running behind me, happy for the exercise. The local station, however, was closed—and completely out of gas, anyway, I was told by a woman passing by on a bicycle. She informed me that the strike had already been going on in this part of the country for several days and there had been no deliveries. The only possibility for gas would be at stations near the *autoroute*, one such station being six miles away. We'd make that easily enough on the fraction of a tank we had left, and so filling our stomachs within the next fifteen minutes became the priority. "Can you suggest a restaurant?" I asked the woman.

"None in this town. And even if there were"—she was calling back as she pedaled on—"there have been no deliveries at all—that includes food."

Even in the unlikely event a French restaurant were to use frozen or canned food to prepare a meal, they wouldn't admit it, so I imagined all restaurants would be closed. "What about dog food? Is there a convenience store or anything at all? My dog hasn't eaten!" I called out to the disappearing figure.

She practically skidded to a stop. "Since when?" she shouted back.

"Days," I lied.

• • •

The stern lecture I'd been given for depriving JP of food was a small price for the lunch we were served. We followed the bicycle to the rider's seventeenth-century estate on the banks of the Sioule, a property she had converted to a bed-and-breakfast.

"Although he doesn't *look* like he's suffering too much," she said, after JP had eaten some organic dog food from her own dog's bowl, along with a raw egg. I told her that what I'd meant was that he hadn't had a *proper* meal in days, what with the strike and all. If there were ever a question of starvation, he'd eat before I did, and I meant it. The woman smiled, forgiving me the earlier exaggeration, and then frowned as JP lifted his leg and soaked her bicycle. "That'll teach me to be the Good Samaritan," she said to him.

"All of the houses on the property come with their own kitchens," she said as she came out of *Le Pigeonnier*, once a dove barn, now a charming rental house on the property with its own yard and view across the river. "So I don't usually prepare meals." Still, she managed admirably, serving me a bowl of *cassoulet de canard* under an umbrella on the patio. "This was supposed to last me a few days, but it's too heavy for me in the summer."

The *cassoulet* was a winter dish, but this stew was light on the gravy and beans, consisting mostly of lean duck breast. It was one of the best I'd had, and it definitely tasted fresh; I asked how she had managed to take delivery of the ingredients. She pointed to a duck pond with three large, healthy-looking specimens gliding along, one of them a male who trailed behind the other two. "*Dorothé*," she said of my dish. Poor Dorothy had been the lone duck's wife.

"You look a little tired, and you won't get far without *pétrole*," the woman told me. "Can I interest you in a room? *Le Pigeonnier* is my favorite—and the only *maisonnette* that hasn't been rented."

I told her that JP's betrothed was waiting in the Var for him, and she nodded, this statement not seeming to require any further explanation. "I'll leave you to your lunch. *Bonne continuation*," she said, and left.

I wanted to feel guilty for eating Dorothy, but I left none of her for JP or Pistou—the woman's boxer, with whom JP had gone off to wrestle and explore. I reclined the cushy lounge chair and lay back, watching the dogs together. I thought about how good it would be for JP to be with other canine companions at the Clix kennel.

In Paris I took him regularly to the Bois-de-Boulogne to play with other dogs, but he didn't engage in the traditional games of ball fetching or tug-of-war. JP genuinely seemed to prefer the more human activities of hanging out in cafés and dining with me. Almost everyone who met him commented on how human he seemed, especially his serious, intense eyes. I closed mine, wondering for the first time if maybe too much was expected of him . . . he was a dog, after all, and maybe he'd enjoy a life in the country, given the chance.

In a reverie between waking and sleep, I recalled the happy day I'd brought JP home with me. On the train to Paris, he'd found a perfect, elevated spot—sitting his eleven-pound body on my right shoulder, and leaning back against the headrest for sup-port—to gaze at the scenery whizzing past the window and ob-serve the heads of other passengers. He'd refused to sleep in the new surroundings, and left his perch only to relieve himself with a visit to the toilet—thanks to Madame Clix, he was already paper-trained; he'd slide down my chest and bite a newspaper or magazine when it was time. With his chubby face, curious mind, and just-sociable-enough manner he'd seduced commuters and stewards alike, one of whom returned to our seat several times with dog biscuits.

He was so tired by the time we got to my six-floor walk-up in Montmartre that he could barely keep his eyes open, but he wouldn't let me carry him upstairs. He'd insisted on stretching his body to its limit, tackling each of the seventy-six steps one at a time by throwing his two front paws upward and out, and then propelling the rest of his body up with his two hind legs. At the sixth floor he hesitated, sniffed, and, guided by his keen olfactory sense, turned left toward my door. Once inside, without the slightest pause he turned, walked down the hallway to the master bedroom (mine), and tried to jump up on the bed. After a few unsuccessful attempts, he let out a small moan of frustration, and I lifted him up. He thanked me with a lick, crawled to the head, plunked himself onto a pillow, and slipped into a comatose slumber until noon the next day. And my apartment suddenly became a home.

• • •

I woke from my nap to find all sixty pounds of JP curled up on the chair with me, snoring, his head resting on my shoulder. Pistou was wide awake, watching us with anticipation; his tail wagged when I opened my eyes.

On the table was a large, dirty plastic container with a note sticking out from under it. I sat up, waking JP. He groaned and opened one eye, not pleased by the disturbance, but when I scratched his belly his tail flew up: As usual, all displeasure vanished in an instant, leaving nothing but unconditional love.

The note said that I could fix myself a coffee in the kitchen, that the *pétrole* should be all we'd need, and that we were welcome to keep the container (best always to have *une réserve*). It was signed "Pistou," and the P.S. said, "Thank you for the fun" in English. The note didn't mention the bag of dog food left for JP.

· · ·

There was a queue of about ten cars at the first station we found open for refueling at the junction of the town of Gannat and the *autoroute*. JP got off the scooter and paced up and down, flirting with the various occupants as we waited our turn. A strong wind had begun to blow, and when a five-euro note slipped out of my hand, JP bolted after it, snatching it up in seconds.

A man who was filling his tank said, "How much do you need? Just that container?" He waved me over. "There's no sense waiting until all those tourists fill up." He had obviously assumed I must be a local with my dog and scooter. A few motorists honked when they saw I was cheating, but the man ignored them and filled my container to the brim. I saw that he had looked at the pump's meter to note the additional cost, and I handed him the five euros, which he took.

"*Merci*," I said.

"*Bon voyage*," he replied, and looked around. "Where's your dog?"

JP was staring at a CAUTION sign, which was dangling from a chain attached to a makeshift barrier blocking the entrance to the freeway. The wind was causing it to sway back and forth. "*Ah bon, il est là*," the man said, relieved that JP hadn't run into the *route nationale*. The sign fell off its chain completely, and JP returned to me and hopped on the scooter. The man shook his head in amusement and nodded good-bye.

Pleased that fate had struck again, I reached into my pocket and squeezed the folded parchment that magically guaranteed our safe passage. The *autoroute* might be blocked to cars, even police cars, but a man and his dog on a scooter could easily slip past the barrier, and we might just have a deserted four-lane freeway at our disposal, at least until the strike ended.

•   •   •

Time flew as did we, and I was now a total believer in white sorcery. The wind was warm, dry, and exhilarating—and blowing from the northwest, an anomaly for this region, I later learned. We were driving southeast, propelled forward at about forty miles an hour, a speed we could never have reached under normal circumstances. JP didn't even complain about wearing his goggles the way he usually did. The days were so long this time of year that there was still a trace of sunlight when we spotted a Formule Une outside Montpellier, the gateway to the magical south.

FATHER KNOWS
BEST AUX BAUX

"Don't exaggerate and lie, *s'il vous plaît*," said Madame Clix.

"I swear to God!" I said.

"What is that supposed to mean? I doubt you're religious," she huffed.

"I'm serious. I'm in Montpellier," I insisted.

She insisted on calling me back on a land line so she could verify that. "Oh. It's come to that," Madame Clix said when the receptionist handed me the phone. "From a five-star Relais and Châteaux to a Formule Une."

She insisted on two other things: that I not attempt to drive all the rest of the way in one day, and that JP stay somewhere decent his last night on the road. I was glad she'd said that because it left us the morning to explore Montpellier, a great college town where I had taken a five-week French immersion course a few years earlier to prepare me for La Sorbonne. It had been my first experience with the south, and I recalled how sad I'd been to leave.

JP and I took water and coffee at the open-air café on the Place de la Comédie, me watching the southern pigeons who looked like doves, JP watching the southern people, with their Mediterranean features, olive skin, light eyes, and animated, outgoing personalities. I spread out our now outdated, useless itinerary to figure out which reservations I'd guaranteed with a credit card and would need to cancel in light of the accelerated journey.

I took care of the hotels we'd left behind in central France, and saw that the only restaurant that had required a deposit was Oustaù de Baumanière in Les Baux-de-Provence, halfway between

Montpellier and *le domaine Clix*, originally booked for four nights from now, our last intended night on the road. I was disappointed since it was one of the most acclaimed restaurants in France; it was nearly impossible to get a table there in the summer.

"*Nous sommes désolés,*" the woman on the phone confirmed, "it is not possible to advance the reservation, but there will be no penalty for canceling and we thank you very much for calling. Perhaps another time. *Au revoir, Monsieur.*"

We sat there, unhurried, through two unsolicited refills (coffee and water), until JP's nostrils began twitching, the town beckoning him. I left some money on the table, and when JP heard the clinking of the coins, he was up and ready to go.

I let JP's eyes and nose guide us through the narrow, whitewashed medieval streets so he could water the occasional palm tree. It felt as though I were discovering Montpellier for the first time, and as if JP had always lived there. This time I wasn't hurrying to a class or busily on the way to a library or bookstore or snack bar. I was seeing things simply, and therefore purely, through his eyes.

JP led us first to a small park that I didn't remember, nestled between two thirteenth-century apartment buildings that were cleaner than most of Paris's or New York's twentieth-century structures. There were no dogs there now, but JP's nose to the ground told me that there had been. Our goal, I had decided, would be for JP to play with another dog at least once every day.

"*On continue ?*" I asked JP when he looked about ready to settle onto a patch of grass. Street cleaners were approaching with pokers, brooms, and dustbins, picking up every last wrapper from the ground. JP looked up at me, wagged, and darted off in another direction. We passed the *boulangerie* where I had once bought my bread every morning. I wanted to stop but didn't because JP was walking quickly, and after all the driving I'd put him through I wanted as much as possible for this to be "his day." But he stopped, just as if I had asked him to, turned around, sniffed, and backtracked straight through the open door. It either smelled interesting, or he sensed it was the familiar place I wanted to be. Either way, he deserved a *baguette*.

"*Merci*," said the woman behind the counter, handing me a *baguette* and some change. "You didn't have him when you were here last," she added, smiling.

I was embarrassed that I had no recollection of the woman, considering that she remembered me amid all the tourists she must encounter.

"You had a—what was it—a small dog, a King Charles, wasn't it?"

Maybe she had me confused with someone else. "No," I said, smiling back.

The woman frowned, confused. "Four, five years ago, wasn't it?"

"Yes, I used to come every morning," I said, "but this is my first dog."

The woman looked seriously put out now, and I could tell she believed I was the crazy one. "*Non*," she said definitively, turned away, and greeted the next person.

Her disapproval—or whatever it was—was palpable, and I left feeling very uncomfortable, as if I should be apologizing.

• • •

We walked as far as we could out onto the Roman aqueduct that extended some two hundred yards into greater Montpellier, until vertigo got the best of both of us, JP turning back first. Walking backward slowly from the edge, I had a view of all of Montpellier and the surrounding hills and plains of the Languedoc region with its olive groves and *mas provençaux*, the stone farmhouses that dot the purple, red, and faded green countryside. The seven-hour drive from the center of France had transported us to an entirely new world, from humid, lush, emerald hills and dales to a multicolored, part-arid, part-semitropical paradise.

"Gray-goh-reeh?" JP was sharp and alert to the French pronunciation of my name before I was, certain that it was directed at me. I could see a dog drinking from a fountain and another chasing birds, but the only humans I could see were those sitting on park benches, oblivious to us.

"Gregory? *C'est vous ?*" The voice came again, unmistakably from below.

JP leapt off the aqueduct onto the ground, and descended to where a woman was making her way up from the grassy slope beneath. She wore a tattered sun hat that looked vaguely familiar, and she carried a small rubber ball. "Bijou still can't fetch for anything!" she said.

It was Mademoiselle Huguenin, one of the professors from the French class who had been like a surrogate mother to her students. She had lived in the dorms, taken breakfast, lunch, and dinner with us, and even gone out to clubs with us, making certain that no one slipped back into his or her native tongue. A wave of nostalgia swept over me, and I hugged her. She responded in an affectionate, but French way—by briefly tolerating the hug and quickly replacing it by air-kissing my cheeks twice each, double the Parisian standard. She dusted herself off and stood back to have a look at me.

"You're all grown up!" she said. "And just look at him! Just look at you!" she repeated to JP. JP smiled and wagged politely, warmly, but, like her, shied slightly away from the squeeze she tried to give him. She seemed very pleased with this behavior.

Mademoiselle Huguenin sat down on the stone step leading to a monument before the aqueduct, and JP and I sat down beside her. She explained that she had married a Lebanese student from that same course, moved to London with him, and had only just returned to Montpellier now that her divorce was final.

"Where *is* Bijou?" she asked herself, looking around. "I'll never forget how attached she was to you, crawling into your lap all the time. Do you know she was depressed for weeks after that course." She paused and added, "I always thought you'd end up in the Midi." Midi is the affectionate name the French give the southern, *méridional* lands of their country.

I explained that I was just passing through, but she didn't seem to hear me and went on talking. "Bijou always hated

Fadi—I should have known." She sighed. "The writing is always on the wall," she said in English, seemingly referring to both of our lives.

It came flooding back to me: Fadi, the handsome man who'd had lots of girlfriends and swore there had been nothing between him and Mademoiselle Huguenin . . . and the little dog who had hated him.

"Bijou!" she called out. "*Viens ici !*"

The dog who had been drinking at the fountain waddled slowly over to us, and then with sudden recognition jumped youthfully into my lap, irritating JP. It was Bijou, the King Charles spaniel, who, of course, had walked to the *boulangerie* with us every morning.

. . .

When we got to her car, Mademoiselle Huguenin and I air-kissed and promised to keep in touch, both knowing we wouldn't. JP and I continued back along the main, cobblestoned street to the Place de la Comédie where we'd left the scooter. I thought about signposts and the writing on the wall that is always there, and was haunted by memories of choices I'd already made in this lifetime that were too late to change. Despite the contentment I felt by being in the Midi, that it was the right place for me to be, something I couldn't discern had been nagging at me all morning, and I was developing an uneasy feeling in my stomach. JP also started getting twitchy.

As we passed the third poster I'd seen for a missing child, Joliane Dupond, aged ten, not seen for six days, a teenaged boy raced by, tearing it off the wall.

"She's safe! Thank God," he cried joyously and kept running. A small piece of the flyer had remained taped to the wall. It read: CONTACTEZ LA PRÉFECTURE DE POLICE. I realized what had been nagging at me.

•   •   •

The most the ATM would allow me to withdraw was three hundred euros, six hundred less than the fine that I was informed had been imposed by the Charité police for riding a scooter without a helmet and not providing vehicle registration to an officer of the peace within twenty-four hours of the infraction. The *préfecture de Montpellier* had successfully pleaded with the Charité police on my behalf for the dismissal of the charge of evading arrest, but the fines for the aforementioned crimes had been doubled and there was no further room for negotiation. At least it turned out that there was no law against transporting a dog.

TRANSACTION REFUSÉE, the screen kept showing when I attempted higher amounts. PLEASE CHOOSE A SMALLER AMOUNT. I returned to the prefecture with the three hundred euros, thinking it would at least suffice for a deposit.

"*Et qu'est-ce que vous voulez que je fasse avec ça ?* What am I supposed to do with that?" the clerk asked. "Consider it a down payment for a loan so that you can skip off again? The only reason you're not in jail is because it's just too much paperwork to exchange between jurisdictions, so consider yourself very lucky."

I pointed out that if I had intended to "skip off" again, I wouldn't have turned myself in. "What if I leave my passport with you until I can come back?" I asked.

The clerk looked at JP's sad, guilty eyes, then at mine, and said nothing; he held out a flat, empty hand, upon which I quickly placed my passport. "Okay, but it's my job on the line if you do try to pull a fast one—I hope you understand *that*," he said. "You've got seventy-two hours. And we don't accept cash, so please remit payment in the form of a *chèque mandat*."

"Can I mail it in?" I asked.

The clerk wrote down his name. "Send it to my attention—along with a self-addressed, stamped envelope if you expect me to send your passport back."

That gave me forty-eight hours to procure a money order, and another twenty-four to post it in from wherever I found myself by then. I had a thought: "I am required to have originals of all my *papiers*, aren't I?"

"*Oui, Monsieur, tout à fait.*"

"But what if I'm stopped and I don't have my passport?"

He thought for a moment, exhaled dramatically, made a photocopy of my passport, and returned the original to me.

"Seventy-two hours," he reiterated.

•　　•　　•

The sun was behind us and hot on my back as we glided along the Chemin d'Arles, the old road leading to Arles. Every truck that was about to pass us honked loudly to warn us—a courtesy we were unused to farther north. In addition, there were no puddles on the side of the road to soak us and blacken JP's coat. There was less water all around, but the vineyards, orchards, and bleached stone houses more than made up for it. And when we did reach the occasional river or pond, the skinny-dipping that seemed the only way to swim was all the more refreshing and cherished by both of us.

We passed a Peugeot 206 parked crookedly off to the side, its tail protruding into the road. On the dashboard was a scribbled note: EN PANNE, broken down. A few miles later a middle-aged man with a bald sunburned head, dressed in a black suit, was making his way along the road rapidly but with obvious discomfort. When he heard us approaching, he turned around and stuck out his thumb, and then, seeing it was just a scooter, turned back around and began to walk even faster.

"Do we have room?" I asked JP as we passed the man and noted his vocation. JP leaned into me, making himself small.

"That's terribly, terribly kind of you," the priest said. "But do you think you can manage it with me on the back as well? It doesn't look very safe. Perhaps if I could just use your phone. Mine is dead, you see."

I gave him my phone but he just stared at it, not knowing what number to dial. "Now what's information?" he asked himself. "Or SOS *dépannage.*" He looked at me. "Do you know?"

I shook my head. "You know," I said, "your car is parked rather precariously back there—it might get hit."

He looked at me gratefully, helplessly. "It is?" he asked.

•   •   •

"There *is* a God," Father Cyril said jokingly as I set his keys on the table and his overnight bag by his chair. "And He is being terribly, terribly kind to me today."

I had left JP in Saint-Gilles, sitting with Father Cyril on a terrace at a café shaded by eucalyptus trees while I went to push the car entirely out of the driving lane and collect the priest's things. The Café des Sports was the only place open on a Sunday, and even Roadside Assistance was not likely to be able to come out today. Father Cyril had left messages for friends and had given my mobile phone as a callback number, so when it rang I told him to answer.

"*Ici l'Oustaù de Baumanière,*" the woman's voice said loudly enough for me to hear. "There has been a cancellation for this evening if you would still be interested."

I could see from his expression that the priest was familiar with the restaurant, and that he was surprised and impressed that they would be proposing a table to disheveled creatures such as JP and me. "*Un instant,*" he said, handing me the phone.

"*Avec plaisir,*" I said after the woman asked if I would be willing to accept the table, with the understanding that there were no rooms available.

"And will you still be just one person and a dog?" the woman asked. It was already nearly eight o'clock, and I looked at the priest. He had an expectant look in his eyes, and I don't know why I felt I should be so presumptuous, but I replied: "*Deux personnes, s'il vous plaît.*"

. . .

"There really and truly is," Father Cyril said when we arrived at the awe-inspiring village of Les Baux-de-Provence. I assumed he meant *a God.* The sun was just setting on the white bauxite mountain into which was carved the tenth-century village of Les Baux. "Oh, we have time yet before dinner," Father Cyril said, in response to my audible intake of breath.

From the plateau at the peak of the hilltop village there was a 360-degree view of the Vallée des Baux, which was a few square miles of bauxite hills, at the feet of which lay olive groves and vineyards, nestled in the Alpilles between Aix-en-Provence and Avignon. It had been a hot day, and the cicadas were still awake, singing, their song echoing all around us. JP made strange whimpering howls, something I'd never heard him do, as if in response to them, and then ran in circles around the ruins of some cave-like dwellings.

"That," the priest said, pointing down into the valley at what looked like a monastery, its grounds lit up with torches, a lighted pool the size of a lake, and a heliport in its own mini forest, "is

Oustaù de Baumanière. Positively my favorite restaurant in the whole world."

•   •   •

Possibly because Père—simply "Father" in French, without the *Cyril*, what felt natural for me to call the priest—and I both ordered the vegetarian *menu des légumes* (at Père's suggestion), or possibly because JP was only offered a bowl of water with no ice (or rice or anything else), JP slept through dinner, totally un-interested. And because one of the first things Père had told me was how grateful he'd been for the vacation from which he was returning, so tired had he been of hearing other people's confes-sions and problems, I made a point of saying very little, and let him do most of the talking.

He also chose the wine (a 1982 Trévallon from Les Baux that bumped the Blagny I'd had at La Côte Saint-Jacques into second place), the cheeses *(un assortiment des fromages de Provence)*, and the *appartement* with the garden for himself (we'd had a choice between that suite and a room, the latter of which I was glad to sleep in, given that it was less than half the price). "These places *always* keep a room or two available for important people," Père told me when I asked how he'd managed to procure them for us. "And who's going to turn away a priest?"

FORCED
AUTHORIZATIONS

It was Monday, *his* day of rest, and so Père had come down to breakfast in the courtyard looking not like a priest but like any other patron in his *vêtements civils*, as he referred to neatly pressed jeans and a short-sleeved dress shirt. Over coffee and warm croissants with lavender honey and kumquat marmalade, Père asked about my journey, wanting to know all the details.

I described everything, including my run-in with the law and the debt I needed to cover. He was an attentive listener, and no matter what he'd said the night before, I got the feeling that he enjoyed hearing people's confessions and problems—but that he might not be so adept at taking care of his own. He had simple, to-the-point comments about stories I recounted. He thought our road trip in general was "emm . . . delightful," our escape from Charité "oooh . . . naughty," the witchcraft "auohh . . . rubbish," our seven-hour drive on the *autoroute* "eeeehh . . . daring."

·   ·   ·

"*Encore refusée,*" said the receptionist, after attempting to swipe my Visa a second time.

"It must be the system," Père said to the girl. Actually, it was because Père had forgotten his wallet in the glove compartment of his broken-down car, and the entire bill of sixteen hundred euros was being charged to my card. "Can't you try putting four hundred euros through at a time?"

"I really shouldn't," she said.

Père winked and she swiped.

APPROVED, APPROVED, APPROVED, and APPROVED—I could hardly believe my eyes.

"Could I trouble you to put another six hundred through?" Père asked her. "Four and two, of course." This time he winked at me. "And if you could reimburse that *en liquide*, I'd be ever so grateful. Just a small cash advance, but it will save us having to go the bank."

The girl said she'd have to ask Monsieur Charial before she could do that. "Oh, do. And please tell him that Father Cyril said hello." Père smiled.

The girl looked in the cash drawer—apparently there was plenty, because she then said, "Oh, I'm sure he wouldn't mind." She accidentally put the six hundred through in one shot, but this time when it was refused, she pressed a key that prompted a message on the computer screen: AUTORISATION FORCÉE ? TAPEZ OUI OU NON. She typed OUI and handed me the slip to sign.

In the garden Père required another espresso and the use of my phone to make two more calls. One was to order a car service to drive him the one hundred miles to his parish; another was to order a parishioner to retrieve his car with a tow truck. I asked him about his almost criminal knowledge of credit card schemes, wondering if I'd ever see his portion of the bill.

"Just one of those little tricks one learns along the way," he said matter-of-factly. "For smaller amounts, no authorization is needed. Four hundred only goes through at the fancier places—otherwise it's only one or two. With our pitiful salaries, the French banking system doesn't usually accord priests sufficient credit limits." In a more serious tone, he said: "But if I were you, I'd curb my spending habits."

When the bill came he said, "Oh, that reminds me . . ." and handed me the six-hundred-euro cash advance from reception, along with a card printed with his name — MONSIEUR L'ABBÉ CYRIL RUTHE-ANIS — and a telephone number. "If you could leave your address on my answering machine. If you write it down I'll only lose it. This way I can send you a check for my half."

As I paid for the coffee, he grumbled that his suite wasn't really worth five hundred euros. "How was your room?" he asked.

    •   •   •

"Now where's that dog?" Père asked as his driver pulled up in a modest Renault Laguna. "JP! Come and say good-bye to me." JP manifested himself quickly from behind a bush and was happy to lick the hand Père held out to him. "Beautiful dog," Père said, as if noticing for the first time. "I know someone who breeds Dalmatians," he added.

"Really? I'm about to breed JP," I said expectantly, thinking, since we were in the neighborhood, that two stud fees could come in handy. He shook his head and laughed: "You don't want to get involved with *this* breeder. She's mad, absolutely mad."

    •   •   •

"You're here! In Provence!" Madame Clix answered, again before saying hello, and before I told her where I was. "Aren't they glorious!" she said. She was referring to the cicadas she could hear in the background that confirmed my whereabouts.

By the time JP and I had taken a swim in the pool, followed by a nap on a hammock attached to two oak trees, it was after noon and quite hot—and the insects had already begun their unmistakable high-pitched chant.

"We're in Les Baux," I said.

"I bet you've gotten fat since I last saw you, the way you've been eating," she analyzed. "But JP is thin, isn't he? We don't want him repulsing his *épouse*."

"Yes," I said.

"But not *too* thin?"

"No, just right."

"I'll be the judge of that," she snapped. "What do you feed him, anyway?" she demanded. "None of that restaurant food, I hope—it's terrible for dogs. Only Spécific brand dry food, isn't that right? That's what we said when you adopted him."

"*Bien sûr*," I lied, and told her we'd be there first thing the following morning—to give me time to pick some up before I saw her.

•   •   •

Père had told me about some prehistoric bauxite caves called the Cathédrale d'Images, and so JP and I went to explore them before we got on the road. They were magnificent, some of the chambers built by humans some ten thousand years ago. The ceilings were dozens of feet high, and the walls colorful with prehistoric etchings and illustrations. I read panels explaining just how far back civilization dated in this part of France, and how the *Templiers*, the Knights of Templar, had set up fort in the bauxite village in the Middle Ages. It seemed that like our witch friends, we too were following in the footsteps of the *Templiers*. Everything echoed, and JP amused himself by bouncing his own loud, coded sounds off the walls in response—which in turn bounced back—and I imagined he was communicating with the spirits of the Knights . . . until the curator asked us to leave since we were disturbing the light show in the next cavern.

•   •   •

It was hard to imagine how anyone could go insane living an *existence paisible* in Provence, unless it was something about the surreal light that inspired artists like Van Gogh, but if I did, I'd want to be put away at Saint-Paul-de-Mausole, too. JP had wanted to stop on the route to Saint-Rémy, and the most beautiful spot happened to be the grounds of the monastery, among *coquelicots*, wildflowers, olive trees, and cypresses—all just as it was more than a century ago.

JP felt a need to mark this territory particularly carefully. I had to bribe him with the promise of goat cheese to get him to hop back on the Vespa. At a little after three, when all commerce would still be closed for lunch, we strolled through the narrow, winding streets of Saint-Rémy, and although JP discovered fantastic old fountains to drink from, shady squares to cool off in, foundations of seventeenth-century muted pastel and homes and chapels to claim for his own and discolor, there wasn't a market to be found open. But JP hadn't forgotten: I'd promised him cheese, and that's what he'd have.

He bolted down an obscure alley after a chic, flirtatious poodle with a rhinestone-studded collar, occasionally looking back at me to make sure I was coming. Remembering my resolve to let him play more, and hoping that he was becoming a more social animal, I followed him and the prospective friend until we all three ended up outside a nondescript storefront without a name, whose facade was being repaired, and whose window shade had been drawn. Both dogs plopped themselves expectantly at the door, unwilling to move or to play.

The poodle barked and a few seconds later the shade was raised and the door thrust open; from inside came the unmistakable stench of ripe cheese. She waltzed in, JP hot on her tail.

"*Salut*, Delphine. Who's your friend?" a man said.

I followed the dogs in, apologizing to the *fromager*, who had opened his glass display and was slicing some Gruyère for Delphine.

"*C'est normal*," the *fromager* said. "They know good cheese when they smell it. Especially that one—she's here every day, like clockwork. In fact, I don't reopen in the afternoon until she wakes me up." He held out a piece of Gruyère to JP, but JP turned away, leaving the *fromager* bemused.

"He's got a preference for goat cheese," I said.

"*Ah bon, un bon petit chèvre . . .*" the *fromager* said, trying to decide which one. "*Sans herbes,*" he concluded, "something not too spicy, a little hard." JP swallowed the entire *crottin* in one gulp. "And what can I get for you?"

"Whatever you suggest," I replied obligingly.

Cheese in France can be a meal in itself, and I was sold enough *échantillons*, samples of various *fromages provençaux*, and bottled water from the *Hautes Alpes* (the *fromager* must have predicted the strike and stocked up) to last us well through to dinner. It was slow moving, though, since JP demanded very regular stops, knowing I was rationing the portions.

I found a post office on the outskirts of Aix-en-Provence where, with the euros Père had creatively obtained for me, I took care of my debt to the French authorities.

"You must have done something very naughty," said the postal clerk when I requested that the *chèque mandat* be made out to the *Trésor public*, the organization to which all fines were paid.

I told her that I was lucky I wasn't in jail.

"*Ma foi !* Oh my!" she said, intrigued. "Well we wouldn't want that, would we?" She smiled at JP. "I don't believe they allow dogs."

For an extra euro and forty-five centimes, she told me, the payment would arrive at the *préfecture* by nine the following morning. I splurged, and JP and I were on our way, our karma in good shape.

We took the uneven shoulder of the *route nationale* N7, from Aix-en-Provence to Le Luc, gliding past the *embouteillage* of frustrated motorists, to the final stretch of the journey, down through the Massif des Maures, a beautiful mountain pass of soft, rounded peaks and forests of chestnut and cork oak, with vineyards covering its plateaus. The fifteen-mile route was incredibly narrow and winding, and it took us a good hour. We were unnerved by the occasional screeching of tires as cars came upon us, averting collision at what seemed to me to be the last second. (Each *département* has its own set of driving rules, and as peaceful as this part of the Var is, its drivers rival the impatience of the Parisians.)

JP and I were both suffering from motion sickness when we arrived at La Garde-Freinet, known as the Island in the Forest, sitting on a long narrow ledge of a pass, overlooked by rocky peaks and the ruins of its ancient fortress. The view of the Maures was spectacular from here, but it went unappreciated on this day—even JP didn't request any cheese when we stopped. The service station did have some club soda in stock for JP's tongue and my stomach, which helped. JP licked some fizz from my hand, and I guzzled the rest.

A man pumping gas with an Irish setter in the back of his jeep told me that the best vet around happened to be the mayor of Grimaud, and that he'd have the widest assortment of dog food. The name *Grimaud* had a certain ring to it that was pleasant to my ears, and since I wanted to be well prepared for the next morning, I convinced JP that as appealing as La Garde-Freinet was, we should hop back on the scooter. Grimaud was only six or so more miles down into the valley, toward the Gulf of Saint-Tropez, and I knew *le domaine Clix* was nestled in an oak forest somewhere between the two medieval villages.

"Can you suggest a hotel in Grimaud?" I asked the man.

"At this time of year, it's not easy finding a room," he said. "I think I've got one left, though." He handed me a card: HOSTEL-LERIE DU COTEAU FLEURI (the hotel on the flowered hillside), CHAMBRES ET RESTAURANT. "Will you be joining us presently?" he asked.

· · ·

"*Monsieur le Maire, bonsoir,*" Monsieur Minard, the owner of the Coteau Fleuri, greeted a man entering with his wife just as we were checking in. "Your table is ready." The mayor was escorted downstairs to the restaurant by a charming, overly sophisticated girl of about thirteen. Monsieur Minard then proceeded to turn away several potential guests apologetically, explaining that he'd just rented his last room—and his last table. Apparently I was expected for dinner, my stomach bloated with cheese or not.

The Coteau Fleuri—and the entire village of Grimaud—was indeed perched on a flowered hillside, at the end of a cul-de-sac whose other occupant was a crumbling stone church from the eleventh century, La Chapelle des Pénitents. There is a tendency to overuse the word *magical* when describing the French countryside, but our arrival into Grimaud could only be described as just that.

•   •   •

We dined light and drank liberally—red wine, I had discovered, aids in the digestion of cheese. JP, on the other hand, refrained even from water. I, at least, left the restaurant less bloated, with a bottle of San Pellegrino for our much-anticipated midnight stroll through the village. We also acquired a bag of much-needed Spécific dog food from a stash the mayor had had in the trunk of his BMW.

We made our way through the tiny, cobblestoned *ruelles* and narrow steps to the ruins of the Château de Grimaud at the very top of the village. The moon was almost full, and the rippling Gulf of Saint-Tropez was ablaze with its reflection in the distance. The breeze was warm and silent, carrying the shooting stars I saw away with it—but not before I wished upon them. We sat on the wall of the château's fortress as below us, candlelight flickered from between the branches of bougainvillea and trellises of grapevines that covered the rooftop terraces of stone Mediterranean houses. Below them, people were sipping *digestifs* and laughing softly, and in our hearts we joined them.

•   •   •

We returned to the Coteau Fleuri at about two. Monsieur Minard was still awake, walking two Irish setters, the second a puppy too small to venture out on its own. The dogs played hide-and-seek on either side of our legs, and Monsieur Minard inquired whether I wanted to spend some more time in the area. If so, he could suggest a few hotels I might try—and another restaurant in the village: Les Santons, since the Coteau Fleuri would, no doubt, be booked.

I thanked him for the suggestions, and then, because I wasn't sure my credit card would ever go through again after its recent usage, and wanted to be prepared in case I needed to find a bank in the morning, I asked if I could pay before going to sleep that night.

"*Si vous voulez.*" Monsieur Minard shrugged, obviously thinking it odd, or at least not very French, to be so anxious to pay a bill. He escorted me to his reception desk and calculated the total—just over a hundred euros. He had a portable card swiper that had to be placed in a cradle that dialed into the Visa center via modem. It took about a minute to get the response: CARTE REFUSÉE. "Err, these things," he growled as if it were the fault of the apparatus and not my card.

"Ahm, could you . . . possibly put fifty through at a time?" I asked.

He shook his head and waved his hand as if to say, *Too much trouble*, and then repeatedly pressed a key on the dialer until the screen read AUTORISATION FORCÉE, and a receipt was printed.

BONBON

"Samuel is jealous and resentful," Madame Clix declared, with the same exaggerated sincerity she inflicted on all her words, as JP smothered her with licks and kisses with a zeal I rarely saw in him; he usually avoided such displays of affection. He had jumped into the air and twirled when he saw Madame Clix, and then practically knocked her over. She, in turn, stared at him, unmoving, in a combination of what seemed to me to be sadness and joy.

"Mon *bébé*, mon *bébé*," she repeated over and over.

Samuel, the chubby, thirty-something caretaker of *le domaine Clix*, sat detachedly caressing his own dog, a miniature collie mix, who was equally unmoved. "You'd think it was her real *bébé*," he said, imitating Madame Clix's high-pitched pronunciation of the latter word. "No offense," he added in my direction with a forced smile.

"None taken," I said.

"Well I *am* offended," Madame Clix said, regaining her balance and composure, and brushing white dog hairs off her black slacks, black sweater, and black scarf. "I won't be ridiculed and mocked!"

Samuel picked up a rake and strutted away, but his dog stayed.

"And take Lucien with you, please!" Madame Clix called to him. Lucien started barking insanely at her, until she waved her fist in his direction, which shut him up instantly.

"The mutt!" she cried.

"Come on, Lulu," Samuel said. Lucien obeyed, but not without one final bark at Madame Clix . . . and a growl at JP.

Madame Clix brushed a few white hairs off my blue T-shirt, and then took my arm, and we walked. "Do you know a good caretaker, preferably one with a little taste?"

I laughed politely.

She looked at me puzzled—had she said something funny? "Do you know," she said, "I think JP is almost as beautiful as his father. May he rest in peace . . . and may God forgive me." She made the sign of the cross, out of order, I thought.

I had only met JP's father fleetingly before the adoption—just so that he could give me the same stamp of approval, a sloppy, wet *coup de langue* across my face, as Madame Clix put it. Any time spent with JP would have depressed Prince, as he had grown attached to all of his departing sons, but particularly to JP. Madame Clix had told me that JP was her only hope for the pro-creation of his bloodline, but since I'd received a death an-nouncement when one of JP's sisters had died in a car accident with her adoptive parents the year before, I thought it was proba-bly a question of fertility, and hadn't realized that Prince des Coeurs was now also in heaven. "*Je suis désolé*," I said, but I don't think she heard me.

The grounds looked better than I remembered, mainly be-cause a large wooden barn that used to loom over the stone buildings on the property, clashing with them in its moder-nity—probably only a century old—had disappeared. Otherwise not a single thing had changed: the flowers, shrubs, and trees, shapely and healthy, were still wild and overgrown, and what I could see of the buildings, overrun with ivy, was beautiful . . . elegant and unkempt, like Madame Clix, and, I thought, meant to look that way.

On a hilltop across from the main house stood a lone palm tree, out of place among the chestnuts and oaks. I'd remembered this from my last visit two years before, and it helped me find my way to the remote hamlet this time. I had gotten a bit lost in the chestnut groves, but the occasional glimpses of the palm tree through clearings had guided us to Madame Clix.

"Did you plant that palm tree?" I asked.

"Ah, *mon palmier,*" she said. "No, it's been here forever. *Depuis toujours.*"

The difference of a few miles and a few hundred feet in altitude from Grimaud and the nearby Côte d'Azur, both lush with palm trees, resulted in a veritable climatic change, and I mused out loud that I didn't think one could be indigenous up here.

"I have a microclimate in my little valley that keeps us warm, but he loves snow, on the rare occasion we have it," she said. The tree did appear to be very healthy.

"Really, how many winters has he survived?" I asked.

"*Depuis toujours,*" she repeated with finality.

Madame Clix hadn't aged since I had last seen her, and she didn't seem any more dramatic or eccentric, but something was different. Whereas before I had found her theatrical, now it was

GREGORY EDMONT

as if the drama were magnified by a more pure emotion that bubbled beneath the surface. She began to walk faster, her hair and clothes flowing, giving the impression that she was floating through the air, toward a path along a stream.

"Please hurry!" she said. "I've got so much to do in preparation for tomorrow." I assumed she was referring to the consummation of JP's marriage to Flirt, but I was wrong.

She led me past a *potager* where all sorts of random vegetables and herbs were growing without any obvious pattern. I could make out celery, lettuce, and rosemary, but nothing else—in fact, the rest might have been weeds.

She must have seen me trying to figure it out. "Have you got a green thumb? Samuel is hopeless and I'm too old." Barely seventy, she didn't seem to lack vitality. "Never mind," she said. "You'll be busy enough as it is, setting up fort." Whatever that meant.

The path continued through a brief but enchanted forest, thick with twisted cork oak and evergreen trees, and JP delighted himself by leaving the path and rolling on his back in a bed of pine needles. "Don't wander, little one," Madame Clix said without looking back at him. "You've got all the time in the world—but I don't. Now come along." JP obeyed instantly, and I got the feeling that if I had wandered she might not have noticed.

We came to a thicket of bamboo trees along yet another stream and then to a clearing that revealed something straight out of a fairy tale: a six-hundred-year-old water mill (according to the date etched into its wheel), which was still struggling to pump, smothered in wisteria and vines, and surrounded by alternate patches of lavender and rosemary.

Of the latter, Madame Clix said, "That's been the extent of my gardening this year."

A stunned "Wow" was all I could manage to say about this paradise, although apparently not enthusiastically enough.

"The least you could do is *sound* appreciative," she said, holding out her perfectly manicured hands. "These blisters are all on account of the little prince. You can thank Samuel for the interior"—she took back her hands—"although I'll have *ma soubrette* go over it again to be sure it's *propre*." She scowled at Samuel's laziness when it came to cleaning.

•   •   •

The inside of the mill—where apparently JP and I would be staying during his honeymoon—was clean enough, but the ground floor didn't have a stick of furniture on it. There was an empty bowl on the counter in the kitchen, and since JP was panting, I tried the water faucet—nothing. "The electricity is *parfaite*, absolutely perfect." There were some very modern light switches that she turned off and on several times to show me. "But the pipes have rotted, all of them. Just as well," she said. "Dogs shouldn't drink water from lead pipes."

"What about me?" I asked.

She looked at me squarely for a moment, deciding whether I was being serious or comical. "You shouldn't either," she said, then, as if she hadn't thought of the other advantages of indoor plumbing I might be concerned about, she added, "There's plenty of it in the stream."

The upstairs had a sitting room with one very large, cozy armchair. It was probably once burgundy, but every inch of it was now covered with white dog hairs, so I gathered it wasn't for my use. There were two bedrooms: one large with an old, uncomfortable-looking twin bed, made up with sheets and a blanket; another small, with a brand-new queen mattress on a wrought-iron frame that barely fit between the walls. The newer firmer mattress was bare except for a bed tray with a dog bone on it, and a thick comforter folded to about the size of a Dalmatian. I was happy to see a modern tiled bathroom with a wide, deep bathtub and separate shower stall, but when I peeked in, Madame waved her index finger at me, indicating that the bathroom pipes were also *foutus*.

Like many of the houses in this part of the world, the mill was built into a hillside with steppes. The large bedroom opened onto a lush garden with a pool of water that was formed where a canal somehow flowed up and met the top of the waterwheel. The surface was covered with flowering lily pads and frogs. I thought this might be where I was expected to bathe until she said, "This is the one place JP isn't allowed. I've spent days on this project and the lilies are just perfect."

A stone staircase led down from the garden into a patch of oak trees where a tiny *maison d'amis* was hidden. The one-room guest house was so overgrown with ivy that Madame produced cutters and chopped her way in through the front door.

"*Voilà.* There's hot water and a nice tub in here," she said, stepping aside so that I could see, but not entering herself.

There was a tub, smack in the center of what was once probably a beautiful room, and two hoselike contraptions attached to the hot and cold water faucets of a sink, covered in cobwebs. "I-it's rather primitive," she admitted quietly, almost disappointed, as if she, too, were just now seeing the place the way it really was, and expecting something else. I saw that she was a woman who lived in the past, and that she was embarrassed.

•   •   •

JP passed in front of Madame Clix, entering the *manoir* as soon as she'd opened the door. She scolded me for his bad manners, but seemed pleased that he felt so at home. He'd had enough of driving, hotels, and visiting, and he needed a place to take a midday nap. He went directly to a clean, silk sofa, with big, soft pillows, and settled in. Unlike the mill, Madame's residence was a haven of comfort, furnished with many expensive antiques. It was meticulously clean and miraculously free of Dalmatian hairs.

Madame had regained her composure. "You look as bad as I feel—weary and fatigued," she said.

"Thank you," I said.

She laughed. "Oh no! Don't tell me you're sensitive and thin-skinned?"

I asked her if she always used two identical adjectives instead of one.

"And you call yourself a writer! If you think *sensitive* and *thin-skinned* mean the same thing, you should certainly change careers," she said.

Before entering a kitchen that was bigger than the entire mill, Madame turned a light on, then off, then on again, very deliberately. While pouring coffee from a French press, she explained the less romantic, nitty-gritty side of canine ovulation—how the percentage of Flirt's dropping eggs was being measured daily by the breeder, and that the window of opportunity would be brief. Indeed, it could open and close within the next several days. The *couplage*, her term for "mating," would take place three times: once every other day.

That could mean we'd have to stay for a couple of weeks. As beautiful as the mill was, I didn't think I'd be comfortable living quite so rustically for so long. "But we raced to get here," I said. "You said it was urgent."

"And it is," she said. When mating dogs, she explained, the *fille* must come to the home of the *garçon*—not just because a female will sometimes not accept a male on her own territory, but also so that the male will have his heart and soul in the mating; a stud in his own territory is more fertile, and there will be more of "him" in the litter. "After all," she pointed out, "it is JP's bloodline that needs to be procreated."

"*Le domaine* must *become* JP's home—and that doesn't happen overnight—or else it will all have been in vain," she said. "Do you know I actually thought of having Flirt brought to you in Paris—that probably would have been easier."

"Probably," I agreed.

"But what would your neighbors have thought?" She found that image very amusing. "But of course my dogs always mate here," she said, looking out the window in the direction of the forest.

I saw that the only way I was going to get through to Madame Clix and make this work was to play her game. "You know, JP is very sensitive to his environment," I said.

"Of course he is!" she said. "That's why I've done all this!"

I nodded, very seriously. "Yes, but I am part of his environment, and he is very in tune with me."

"As it should be," she concurred.

"JP can only feel at home if I do," I said, and I could see I had her full attention. "And I'm afraid I could only feel comfortable with indoor plumbing."

•　　•　　•

While the plumber tore into the innards of the mill, Samuel and I went through the attic of the *manoir*, sifting through the dozens of antiques that had once furnished it. Madame and JP napped. The commotion was too much for them. My experience with Parisian plumbers and electricians had been unlucky, especially when they were called on short notice, and so I was astounded and comforted that after several hours of hoisting and carrying furniture I was able to soak in a hot bath that evening, alone in my mill with JP.

·   ·   ·

"He's obviously not familiar with this particular *flavor* of Spécific," Madame said at dinner as JP stared blankly at the bowl that was placed in front of him. "What flavor do you *normally* give him?" she asked accusingly.

"It varies," I said.

"I suspected and knew it!" she cried. "There is but *one* flavor! I'll bet the only thing that varies is this poor dog's *nutritional intake*." She sighed as if she'd lost a battle, and then opened the refrigerator. "*Bon*," she said. "What does he eat? Just tell me and admit it. It's best not to modify his diet at this stage."

We followed her to the kitchen and I explained that up until our departure, JP had always eaten freshly steamed rice, cottage cheese or *crème fraîche*, broccoli, and a very small amount of boiled chicken breast.

"White or brown rice?" she asked.

"White," I said.

"Hmmph," she breathed. "Where did you learn about that *régime* ?"

I told her that I had done a bit of my own research on how to raise JP, and that I'd contacted the Dalmatian Club of Paris for literature. When I told her that I also gave him calcium and multivitamin supplements, she rolled her eyes and shook her head. *"Typiquement américain*, those vitamins," she said, but she was obviously impressed, and admitted that such a nearly vegetarian meal was ideal for Dalmatians.

"I suppose he'd like it served on an *assiette ?*" she asked.

I replied that he didn't need a fancy plate.

$$\bullet \quad \bullet \quad \bullet$$

After Madame had prepared JP's dinner, she and I sat down in the dining room, where we were served by her Portuguese *soubrette*, a quiet woman of about forty. "This is Anne-Marie," Madame said. "In case you need anything."

The woman smiled politely. "Anna María, *Monsieur*," she said, correcting Madame's francophone pronunciation of her name. "Madame," she continued, placing a giant, rare steak with béarnaise sauce before Madame, and then an arugula salad with lemon, olive oil, and Parmesan cheese before me.

"I dine very simply—I hope you don't mind," she said, pouring me a glass of 1982 Beychevelle.

"No, this is perfect," I said. "Aren't you having salad?"

Madame contorted her face. "I detest it—I can't eat anything leafy and green," she said, swirling her Bordeaux and holding the glass to the candlelight to inspect the color and robe.

Even though Madame didn't seem to eat quickly, whereas I thought I tended to, she had finished her steak and wiped up every drop of béarnaise sauce with bread before I started on mine. She was then served a Mars bar.

"Don't worry," she said. "You'll have a proper dessert." She looked at her watch. "Anne-Marie, has Dominique called?" she shouted.

"No, Madame!" Anna María shouted back.

Madame rolled her eyes. "Not that she'd bother to answer the phone," she said, just as Anna María entered with my steak, slightly less rare. "Dominique is my veterinarian. He said he might stop by to have a look at JP."

"Madame—" I started.

"*Bonbon*," she corrected me. Upon hearing the word for "candy," JP awoke from a sound sleep and sat by Madame. "*Il est trop, celui-là*. He's just too much, that one," she said, delighted. Then, admonishing me, "And you, please stop calling me Madame! You make me feel mature and old! Madame this, Madame that. Call me Bonbon, for God's sake." To Anna María she said, "Bring Gregory some more béarnaise sauce—what's he supposed to do with those few drops you've dribbled on top of the meat?"

Anna María nodded. "*Oui*, Madame."

"And bring the little prince a piece of steak, too, would you?" She smiled at JP, who looked up at her and smiled back, tilting his head to the side so that she could scratch his neck. "*Il est vraiment trop*, he is really too much," she said. "Now what were you going to ask me?"

"Well—where are all your dogs? I know JP's father is gone—I'm very sorry—but what about his mother? And didn't you keep two from JP's litter, a girl and a boy?" She looked at me strangely, coldly, as if she thought I was judging her. "That's a lot to care for, there's no reason you should have—I just thought there'd be Dalmatians running around all over the place like the last time we were here."

She continued to stare at me another moment, and then suddenly began to hyperventilate. She reached out with one of her hands and squeezed mine, and put the other on her chest. This was not an act—she was having some kind of attack. I stood up and reached for a glass of water but she waved it away, knocking it out of my hand and sending it smashing to the floor. Anna María came running in just as Madame let out a bloodcurdling scream.

Anna María poured some water onto a napkin and wet Madame's forehead with it, then leaned down and held her. "Oh Bonbon, *pauvre Bonbon, ce n'est pas de votre faute*—it's not your fault. Tomorrow's a new chapter, Bonbon."

Bonbon put her head onto Anna María's bosom and wept.

RESTING IN PEACE

"QUELLE TRANSFORMATION !" Anna María said as I opened the door the following morning, speaking of the now exquisitely furnished mill. She set down a sweet-smelling straw basket on the kitchen table and then walked from room to room, upstairs and down, before finally returning and sitting at the table.

She looked at me, still standing, and then at the basket. "*C'est très décontracté ici,* we're very casual here—you should make a habit of helping yourself," she said, removing a still-warm croissant and *pain aux raisins* for my breakfast. Things at the *manoir* were not what I'd call casual for Anna María, and so I understood her message that I shouldn't expect her to wait on me hand and foot as well.

"You can't imagine what it has been like these past few months. I really thought we were going to have to—" she paused, "—*do something* with Madame."

I opened the door to let JP out, and Anna María stood up to leave as well, seemingly unprepared to offer further explanation, but I wasn't going to let another day pass without one.

Before allowing Anna María to help her up to her room the night before, Madame had insisted that JP and I stay for our dessert and coffee, making Anna María promise to be sure we did. Madame had apologized over and over as Anna María led her away. The apologies were directed at me, but were too profound for something as inconsequential as cutting short a dinner. JP was whimpering because Madame was whimpering, and he had tried to follow her upstairs.

"*Non,*" Madame had said weakly. "Stay with Gregory—he's your *papa* now. I don't deserve you." At the foot of the staircase, before climbing, Madame had switched the lights on and off several times to make sure they were in working order.

Anna María had simply obeyed Madame's orders, serving dessert in a silence that had seemed inappropriate for me to penetrate.

This time I was determined to comprehend.

"You mean, you don't know *l'histoire* ?" she asked incredulously. "But you have come all the way from Paris!"

"To breed my dog," I said.

Anna María shook her head. "To attend a funeral."

•   •   •

Nearly three months before, on April 10—coincidentally, the day before JP's birthday—there had been a terrible accident, Anna María told me. Madame's dogs, the loves of her life, died. The warm, vivacious, kindhearted Madame Clix disappeared with them, and a fearful, unstable, and distant woman took her place.

Madame had planned a birthday party on April 11 for the two puppies she'd kept. It was to be the most important day in their lives, their second birthday, the day they would come of age—and become eligible for breeding. "You're a man now," Madame had written in the birthday card she'd sent JP.

Normally the dogs had the run of the property—except during mating season, when Madame kept the boys sleeping in the house with her, and the girls in the barn—but because the house was being decorated for the birthday festivities, with Anna María and Samuel putting up banners and setting out party favors, she had confined all the dogs to the barn. A strong *mistral* wind had risen late that evening, and a faulty cable outside was tossed around, creating sparks and igniting some hay in the loft while Madame was out to dinner in Grimaud.

"Madame knew there was a short because the lights in the barn had been flickering for weeks," Anna María said, shaking her head at the futility of it. By the time Madame had returned from her meal, the barn had burned to the ground.

"It was your thank-you card that snapped her out of it, you know—just long enough for her to contact you," Anna María continued, not seeming to notice my silence.

I think I had gone pale from the nausea I was feeling. I couldn't respond; I just shook my head.

"No, really," she said. Apparently Madame had always thought that *JP* stood for something like "Jean-Paul" or "Jean-Pierre"—"strange choice for an American, not to mention trite," Madame had once said to Anna María—but when I responded to her birthday card, I intentionally wrote JP's full name out, and included a photo. After only two days of living with JP, I knew that the first name I'd chosen for him—Skip—wasn't noble enough. With the help of my Croatian neighbor (who was fluent in the ancient Dalmatian dialect), I decided on Jarny-Prince, a name meaning "Prince of Springtime," which I thought would suit him and Madame Clix—and apparently it did.

"She saw that JP was a Prince, too." Anna María smiled for the first time. "Madame thought that the Prince des Coeurs was trying to tell her something, through your JP."

•　　•　　•

I ran outside to find JP as soon as Anna María left. He was wading in the stream, watching birds who were dancing from tree to tree. When he saw me coming, his eyes lit up and he leapt out of the water onto me. He always senses when I need some attention. I rolled around on the ground with him, and he pinned me down playfully and licked my face. I couldn't imagine how Madame Clix was managing to get through her loss—or how I would survive one day without JP—and for the first time in years a tear rolled down my cheek, just at the thought of it.

•　　•　　•

"Of course Madame was selfish before, too—" Anna María said an hour later, now seemingly purged of sorrow, when she returned to the mill with a pair of long black trousers and a sewing kit. With one arm she swept the kitchen table of toast crumbs, then set the items on it. "That's because she's always been *une excentrique* . . . but now she's just plain crazy."

People who don't love dogs just cannot understand, I thought.

She shook her head again. "Madame only announced the date of the *cérémonie* after she knew you and your dog would be here! Yet everyone who ever laid eyes on the dogs is expected to drop everything and come." Part of Anna Maria was enjoying the drama of it all. "She saw her priest and he suggested it! He said it would be good for her to have *finalité*. He's as loony as she is— just wait until you meet him. Imagine, a funeral for dogs. I am not prepared to attend such a *charade*, I can tell you that." She made the sign of the cross.

Yet she was prepared to alter a pair of the late Monsieur Clix's trousers to fit me so that I could be appropriately dressed in a dark suit, as Madame had requested of the attendees.

• • •

The funeral began at the site of the tragedy; the charred foundations of the barn were still visible. The French, especially the southern French, do not shy away from grief. When loss befalls them, they face it head-on—living and breathing it, sometimes until it consumes them, almost to the point of morbidity. But perhaps that is an effective tool in the healing process. They always seem to snap out of it, often in time for a repast.

Madame stood by an intact but blackened cross that had apparently survived the fire. She was utterly composed, but I could see that she was feeling every bit of her emotion from the night before, less the angst, and in a strange way it made her more radiant. I had expected her to be pale, disheveled, dramatic.

Instead she was very tidy, dressed in a simple black pantsuit, wearing just the right amount of makeup to appear presentable and elegant. This truly was not about her; it was about the five lost souls, the cinders of their former bodies in individual urns on the ledge of a brick chimney that had once been inside the barn and was now a shrine. In the center of the shrine was a blow-up photograph of Prince des Coeurs. He was the spitting image of JP, and I suddenly felt more connected to—and more troubled by—this event.

A crowd of about a dozen people and half a dozen dogs, four liver Dalmatians and one chocolate Labrador, began to arrive on the path leading from the *manoir*. The people were dressed in black, except for one bizarre-looking woman wearing a short brown dress and bright pink blush. Samuel stood at the back of the crowd, his black overalls and work shirt covered in dirt, as if he'd only just taken a break from working. Notably absent were Samuel's dog, Lucien, and Anna María. Madame closed her eyes, silent, waiting for the people to gather around. When she spoke, it was with a humble, commanding, and steady voice.

"I'm not going to bore you with long speeches and make you suffer all this bloody *symbolism* for more than a few minutes," Madame said, self-mockingly, of the urns sitting on what looked like the mouth of a giant oven. A few people laughed somberly. "Prince touched many of your lives in almost as profound a way as he touched mine. He and his children were a staple in our small group of friends. Not a single one of you forgot to buy birthday gifts for the brood." She paused before saying, "And for heaven's sake, don't throw them out yet—I haven't given up on the next generation!"

There were a few more laughs, and one or two even put their hands together to clap, but Madame became serious again.

"When Prince met Charmeuse and their children were born there was never a more perfect family, never a happier *époque* at *le domaine*—all shattered, horribly, by me."

A few people uttered the word *non*, but she held up her hand and nodded sadly. "And worse, I then deprived you of the right to mourn those innocent lives by retreating the way I have, wallowing in my own sorrow. Please forgive me." She then looked at the urns. "*Pardonnez-moi.*"

"I hope you're all up to a walk to the cemetery," a familiar voice said.

There was a chorus of *oui*s and several said, "*Mais bien sûr,* but of course."

A priest in a cassock walked up to the shrine, about to pick up an urn, when a woman said: "*Monsieur l'Abbé, non !* Let us carry them."

The priest turned around, willingly empty-handed. "If you insist," he said. It was Père.

•   •   •

It was quite a hike up to the top of the rocky, bushy, thorny hill on which stood Madame's *palmier*. The tree grew atop a mound of earth around which a natural pool swayed and bubbled from an underground source that both watered and kept the palm tree's roots warm and insulated. Behind the tree, where the terrain was flat, lay a small cemetery for the dogs of *le domaine Clix*, complete with gravestones. There were five recently dug graves just big enough for the urns, and in front of them was a bucket with fresh white water lilies.

JP and I, and an elderly woman we had helped (practically dragged) up the hill, were the last ones in the procession, and Madame and Samuel were already placing the last of the urns into the graves.

Père spoke first. "I have blessed each and every Clix beast since my tenure in the Var. If my memory serves me well, that would be two dozen dogs, three or four cats, two goats, a cow, and an ass."

"Oh, Happy, *quelle magnifique bête*," someone said of the ass.

"But this is decidedly the first time I have ever done the obsequies. I'm both honored and saddened to be here." Many people made the sign of the cross.

"God is many things, to many people of many faiths," Père went on. "But what is He to a dog? Could it be that a dog sees God more clearly than we do? After all, God is in everything, in the things we see and touch and smell. God has blessed us with those glorious senses not only so that we can look after and protect ourselves, but so that we might use them to live full and passionate lives. We forget the importance of those senses, often forget to use them, but a dog never—not for a single moment of any day—forgets them." He paused while people absorbed this.

"Love," he said somberly. "Love is God's greatest gift to mankind, and I daresay that it is a gift He has bestowed upon beasts as well, and especially upon dogs. A dog's love for his owner is *absolument simple*—pure and unconditional, the way God wants us to love. The ability to love unconditionally comes naturally to babies and puppies—only, unlike babies, puppies don't ever forget it. Whereas a dog's love grows more pure as he ages, man's love often becomes complicated, sometimes with the most demanding of conditions attached to it, burdening it. We must dig deep into our hearts every day, to remember how to love. And sadly, the best most of us can ever hope for is to *aspire* to love as a dog loves." I noticed a few heads nodding.

"And so what is a dog to God? Well, if God's greatest gift to us is love, if God *is* love, then a dog is undoubtedly one of God's finest instruments. A dog's life is short, too short, most of you would agree. Why should God grant us such love, only to take it away from us after only a few short years? I don't have all the answers and don't pretend to, but I do know that such love for a dog transcends our existence here on earth.

"Tragedy is something else, another cross many of us must bear in this lifetime, and I can only hope that you will share in my faith that God does have a larger plan. Perhaps it is to remind us of our true feelings, feelings we often take for granted. We must remember that the pain, the guilt we feel when we lose our loved ones, man or beast, are outweighed by the joy we have known from living with them on this earth, and it is nothing compared to the joy we will know again with them in the hereafter.

We must do our loved ones justice by honoring only the joy they have brought us. We must bury the pain along with their ashes, so that we can share the joy and love with the legacy they will have left behind. Not to do so would be an even greater tragedy." Père picked up a lily and tossed it into the first grave. "May Prince, Charmeuse, Jarnac, Jeanne—"

"Jeann*ine*," Madame corrected.

"—Jeannine, and Jolie," Père continued. "May they all rest in peace."

"*Qu'ils reposent tous en paix*," the mourners echoed, and bowed their heads.

•　•　•

"Anne-Marie!" Madame shouted as we approached the *manoir*. She counted aloud the dogs' heads. "We're having eleven people and *un-deux-trois-quatre-cinq-six* dogs for lunch."

"*Mon Dieu*," a worn-out Anna María could be heard saying through an open window. Madame needn't have worried about JP feeling at home. Upon hearing the word *lunch* he instantly moved to the head of the crowd and was the first at the door. Guarding it, he waited expectantly until Madame reached it. I hurried ahead myself, to make sure he didn't offend anyone, but they all seemed content for him to lead the pack.

"*Précieux*," Madame said to me, speaking of JP. He allowed her, Père, and me to enter first, then crossed the threshold himself. Madame immediately reached for the light switch, but she let her hand linger for a moment until Père covered hers with his own. She entered the room without testing it.

●　　●　　●

The house was not festive, but the *repas* was fit for a king. The long dining room table had eleven place settings, and the first course of *tarte d'asperges* with *foie gras* had already been served. Two bottles each of Domaine Ott white and rosé were being chilled, and six bottles of Domaine de la Bernarde red were on a side table, opened to breathe for the main course.

Across from the table were six pottery bowls, set upon wooden footstools so that they were about eight inches off the ground. The first one contained steamed rice, cottage cheese, broccoli, shredded chicken breast, and a garnish of a small piece of *foie gras*. Anna María was pouring two cups each of Spécific dog food into the other five bowls. The chocolate Labrador and one of the Dalmatians tried to get to the first bowl—obviously JP's—at the same time, and a scuffle ensued.

Madame cried *"Non !"* Uncharacteristically, JP barked firmly.

The two guilty dogs cowered, slinked to other, as-yet-unfilled bowls, and waited.

Madame smiled. *"Très bien, JP."*

JP beamed at her, not noticing the glare emanating from my direction, and started to eat. After a few seconds, he lifted his head and turned his blameworthy eyes slowly in my direction, inclining his head. He was ashamed that I was disappointed in him, and he stopped eating. JP was not a selfish dog, and was only doing what he thought would please Madame: trying to keep the peace. I was overcome with two sentiments: guilt with the realization that my flawed human love for him might be conditional . . . and profound gratitude to this God of dogs and men that He deemed me worthy of the gift of JP.

OPENING DOORS

"ARE YOU ANY good at *débroussaillage* ?" Madame called out to me from beneath the trellis. I wasn't completely awake, wasn't sure what *débroussaillage* was, and definitely wasn't up to it, whatever it was. I squinted at my watch and saw that it was almost ten. JP opened an eye, took one look at the state I was in, and closed it again. He had rejected the mattress intended for him as soon as Samuel and I had installed an even more comfortable one for me. "I'll take that as a yes," Madame said.

.   .   .

For half of us the post funeral party had lasted until the wee hours of the morning; for the five who had brought dogs, it had ended at a more decent hour sometime before dinner, either because they had to put their dogs to bed or because they were tired of hearing about JP, whom Madame now referred to as her *ange*. The six who remained ate little and instead spent most of the evening emptying Madame's *cave à vins.*

After having a few glasses himself, Père recounted his meeting with me as proof that God gives us signs proving His existence. "As many of you know," he started off, "I have only just returned from holiday in the Camargue. Of course, some of you *don't* know because you don't stay in touch with me. On the road from Montpellier to Arles, my car broke down."

"Again!" someone exclaimed.

"Yes, again. I find that it inevitably does break down when I am driving through life too quickly, without stopping to notice signposts—especially when they say things like BROKEN GLASS AND NAILS AHEAD—and to appreciate what is around me. As I walked to the nearest town, in sweltering heat, who should pass me but a young man on a scooter, heavy with bags strapped to its sides and a very large dog on the footrest." There were some admiring oohs and ahhs. "They stopped to see if I needed help. And as God would have it, they happen to be the man and dog sitting opposite me just now."

Although I had said very little all evening, this little bit of destiny bonded JP and me instantly with the other guests, more so than did the fact that I had adopted one of Charmeuse's litter. Because of that, before the night was through, JP and I had enough invitations for meals and lodgings to last us our entire stay. Whenever an invitation was extended, Madame sneaked me either a subtle nod or shake of her head to advise me whether I should consider it or not. It became too confusing, and so I accepted only the first one that met with a very pronounced nod of approbation: from the mayor of Grimaud—"my veterinarian, Dominique" to Madame—with whom I was of course already acquainted.

•   •   •

"Where's JP? Is he with you?" Madame was obviously not going to give up. JP yawned, sighed, and stretched, realizing, too, that our remaining seconds in bed were numbered.

"Yes! He's right here," I shouted. I knew instantly from Madame's silence that she was disappointed he hadn't rushed down to greet her. "I've got the bedroom door shut," I lied. "He's scratching to get out." JP looked at me sideways, knowing I'd uttered some kind of untruth.

"Oh!" Madame said gleefully. "Well, do let the little man out!"

We got out of bed and went downstairs. I was in a thick cotton bathrobe that Anna María had delivered along with fresh linens the day before.

"Go figure," Madame said, when she saw me. "She's too pious to attend a religious ceremony honoring the passing of a dog but she's not above stealing! That's my late husband's robe you've got on!"

"I had no idea, Madame," I apologized.

Madame folded her arms and squinted her eyes at me. "You know, you seem to be a very well-brought-up young man, but you've nonetheless the tendency to be disrespectful and rude."

"I'll take it off right away." I turned to go back into the mill, assuming I had somehow slighted the memory of another of her deceased.

"Don't be ridiculous," she said. "It looks better on you than it ever did on him. *I mean,* it's very disrespectful to stand before a woman whom you refer to as *Madame* dressed only in a robe — and extremely rude to refer to a woman as *Madame* when she has explicitly asked you not to." She waved her finger at me teasingly.

"Bonbon," I said.

"That's better." She smiled. "Now about that *débroussaillage.* Samuel is just hopeless at it. He's not nearly as muscular as you." I wasn't particularly muscular, but a compliment intended for a human, coming from Bonbon, was particularly effective and she knew it. (Not to mention the fact that by the time I finished the *débroussaillage*—which turned out to be the annual clearing of woods around houses in this part of the Var, as required by fire hazard regulations—I had actually defined quite a few more muscles. "You see?" she said, squeezing my bicep on the fourth day of all-morning work cutting back the thick shrubs and dried branches some twenty yards into the forest on all sides of the mill. "I told you you were muscular. And you've got no one but me to thank.")

"You were quite a hit last night," Bonbon said as she led me to the toolshed to explain the task at hand, after I had made us some coffee in the kitchen. "I think Marie-Josée even has a bit of a crush on you."

Marie-Josée was the bizarre woman dressed in brown (*liver brown*, Madame later informed me, in honor of the departed). She was otherwise an attractive, unattached thirty-something lawyer with a chocolate Labrador, and I recalled that when she had drunkenly plopped herself in the middle of the sofa JP and I were slouching on, Madame told her never to come between a man and his dog.

"It was especially endearing when Père Cyril recounted the little *histoire* of his encounter with you," she said. "That really is quite incredible. How is it you didn't even think to tell me?"

I told her that I'd never made the connection—and I hadn't. Père had proffered very little pertinent information about his own life. "His *carte de visite* didn't even have an address on it," I said. "And of course I didn't want to pry."

Bonbon laughed. "*C'est un cas, celui-là.* He's a case, that one." She looked at JP. "But I do find it odd that he didn't notice the resemblance, that JP was a veritable double of Prince," she added, slightly paranoid.

"He did say he knew a wonderful breeder of Dalmatians," I amended, but not very effectively.

She smirked at the fib and handed me a pair of cutting shears. "You're *poli* for an American," she said.

•   •   •

JP and I took the afternoon to do some wandering together. I was anxious to see Grimaud again, so we climbed on the Vespa and set off. As used to all kinds of weather as we were, both of us appreciated riding under the ever-present sun of Provence as we made our way through the hills—there hadn't been a cloud in the sky since we'd arrived. At the foot of the village JP stood up on the scooter, something he knows he's not supposed to do, but as hard as I tried, I couldn't push him back to a seated position.

"What is it, Japes?" I asked him. He was staring up the hill at something. I accelerated, and when we got to the top I saw two very fine female Brittany spaniels sitting on the small porch of one of the village houses. The girls were staring at JP, and there was no mistake about it, JP was *showing off.*

"Mais quel culot !" a woman from inside called out. "Proud of himself, isn't he?"

I told JP to sit, and finally he did. "I think he's flirting with these beauties," I said.

A rather large woman who must have been nearing eighty years of age opened the door, exiting with much difficulty because of her swollen legs. *"Quel amour !"* she said of JP, and then added politely to me, realizing she should greet me as well, *"Pardon. Bonjour, Monsieur."* She looked at me closely. "Are you from here?"

"No, I wish I were," I said.

"Well, why aren't you, then? Take it from me: Life's too short to not be where you want to be."

• • •

"Every village has got one," Madame Poulin said.

"What's that?" I asked.

"An old-timer like me who knows everyone and everything about everyone." I gathered that she wanted to know even more people and even more things. When I told her where I was staying, she said of Bonbon, "Oh! I could tell you things about *her!* Quite a *bombe* in her day." Madame Poulin was the village gossip, but she was also very well liked—or else very much feared. In the twenty minutes JP and I spent talking with her, she must have been greeted warmly and kissed by half a dozen passersby.

She waddled inside and back out twice with huge slices of non-French cheese for JP. "I can't afford to dole out the nice stuff, so packaged Swiss will have to do." JP seemed to like Swiss as much as goat cheese, and he rewarded her with kisses, while her own dogs drooled. "My goodness, he's *un amour*," she said again.

I asked her what I should see in the village, and she suggested all three churches, because she was a very devout Catholic, herself. I told her I had already seen la Chapelle des Pénitents when I had stayed at the Coteau Fleuri.

"Hauh! Does Madame Clix know you stayed *chez lui* ?" She laughed.

"No, why?" I said.

"She can't stand him! Because he hunts boar with his dogs." She shrugged. "Her dogs are too good for that—but I've nothing against hunting, myself. Dogs were meant for man—and men hunt."

I told her that I was having dinner at Les Santons that evening.

"*Ooh là là*," she said with familiarity, as if we'd known each other for years. "Aren't we *chic*. Next you'll be telling me it's with the mayor—that's his haunt, you know, although sometimes he dines at the Coteau Fleuri for a change of taste. You'll probably see him there."

"Probably," I said.

"Well I don't want to ruin your dog's appetite, so I won't give him any more—but my door is always open, just ask anyone," she said. JP kissed her again.

On the way to the church, we discovered the open-air market on the Place Vieille, the old village square. *Marchés* are a morning event, even in Paris, but especially in warmer climates, and here in the hot sun the market was dwindling. Only a butcher, a refrigerated cheese truck, a fruit and vegetable stand, and a fresh flower table remained.

"*Hé,*" a man said. "He's too thin, that dog. I'll tell you what: You buy one *saucisson* for yourself, and I'll throw one in free for the pooch *gratuit.*"

I told the man I'd pass on the offer, but thanks. He scowled at me and made a comment I couldn't hear, but threw a *saucisson* to JP anyway. As I knew he would, JP sniffed it, left it, and walked away.

"*Ce n'est pas gentil, ça.* That's not very nice," the man said, as if he'd expected me to pay for the *saucisson.* From the look on her face, the woman selling fruits and vegetables next to him concurred — until I bought some fresh *melons* from Cavaillon.

"*Un touriste ?*" I heard the man ask her suspiciously as we walked toward the flowers.

"I don't know, probably," the woman said. "I heard that Clix lady is breeding again — maybe it's something to do with her."

The village houses were even more beautiful in the day, sun-drenched and colorful, with blooms of potted flowers streaming from windowsills and rooftops. Down a small street across from the church, we saw a village mansion under construction. A stunning, tall, blond woman opened the door, coughing, releasing a cloud of dust.

"Do you speak French?" she asked me in accented English.

"*Oui*," I responded in French.

"Oh good," she said, "could you please come in and tell the workers they're knocking down the wrong wall and that the kitchen is caving in?"

The dust didn't interest JP, and he waited on the doorstep. From the outside, it looked like any of the other—admittedly fine, but small—village houses; inside, however, it was a veritable palace. We went through the kitchen (which was, in fact, caving in from the ceiling) and upstairs where the workers were drilling and sledgehammering.

"Excuse me!" the woman called, but they didn't seem to hear.

"*Excusez-moi*," I said, in what I thought was a quieter tone. They stopped instantly.

"*Oui ?*" the foreman said.

"Apparently you're knocking down the wrong wall," I said.

"Which one are we supposed to knock down?"

"I'm not sure, but the kitchen is collapsing." The three men looked at one another.

The foreman asked, "Are you sure that beam wasn't holding the ceiling up?"

Another man shrugged. "*Pretty* sure."

"Inconveniences are to be expected," the foreman said to me, cheerfully enough. He continued, addressing the woman, as if this were something she should have thought of before moving to Provence: "These village houses are money pits."

It seemed that if rebuilding the kitchen was now necessary, the workmen would consider it all part of the job—and part of the tab.

•   •   •

On our way back up to *le domaine Clix* we stopped by Madame Poulin's to give her some French cheese I had bought at the *marché* for her two dogs. Madame Poulin sniffed, it, in a way expressing appreciation for "the real thing," and took it gratefully. She promised to give it to Jolie and Belle when they returned from their walk. All the while, though, she stared at the flowers I had bought for Bonbon.

Madame Poulin informed me that a French entertainment mogul had just bought the house under construction for his Swedish mistress because Grimaud was a discreet village, one of those French paradises that are such well-guarded secrets where one can do what one wants, unnoticed. If he only knew.

As we pulled away, I smiled and waved at Madame Poulin, who was standing in the doorway, still looking at the flowers. I stopped, got off the scooter, and unstrapped them. "Oh, I almost forgot," I said, handing her the bouquet.

She said that JP and I were angels fallen straight out of the sky, and that Jolie and Belle would be thrilled with our thoughtfulness.

She put the flowers in water and the French cheese on a plate. I had a feeling that Jolie and Belle would only get what was left of the Swiss cheese, and I also had a feeling that Madame Poulin would probably make a very good ally.

"*La porte est toujours ouverte !* My door is always open!" she called from her window as we rode away.

• • •

"*Normalement,*" said the mayor as he spooned some caviar onto a blini, "a fertility test is done."

"How?" I asked, meaning what kind of blood test.

"Manually," he replied, shrugging, meaning how the sperm was extracted. He laughed at the look on my face. "Most dogs prefer a feminine hand, so I leave the task to my *infirmière.* He'd react the same as he would if it was a *chienne,* a female dog . . . and he knows what *that's* like."

He waved to Madame Girard, the blond woman who seemed to be in charge of the restaurant. He had tried to get her attention several times, but she was busy dazzling patron after patron, man and woman alike, with her manner, person, and piercing blue eyes. I wondered only until my first course of *Risotto de Homard* arrived if she might be the reason why every table in the establishment was taken. Then of course I discovered, as everyone else already knew, that Les Santons was the gastronomic jewel of the Côte d'Azur.

"Dominique"—Madame Girard addressed the mayor informally, as nearly everyone else did—*"qu'est-ce que je peux faire pour toi ?* What can I get you?"

"A bit more *fromage frais*," he said in a hushed tone, "and maybe if you could scrape a few more grains of rice off the bottom of the pot, *ma chère.*"

Madame Girard nodded with a warm apologetic smile, as if she had overlooked something, *"Tout de suite,"* she said.

The mayor gave me an envelope containing several pages of French text of homeopathic cures he swore by—the translation of which I had promised him in exchange for the bag of Spécific dog food from my first night in Grimaud, and tonight's dinner. His *cabinet* spent a lot of time trying to explain to the many foreign transplants in the area why he didn't want to simply prescribe the antibiotics they requested to treat their pets, and he thought it would be easier if he could provide some documentation in English.

JP had fallen asleep after his first serving of rice and *fromage frais* and looked as though he thought he was dreaming when seconds were delivered by Jean-Louis, the sommelier, along with another silver bowl of ice water. He looked at me for approval, stretched, and dug in.

When JP had finished, Madame Girard came up and said loudly, "Is this the prodigy the village has been whispering about?" I smiled, a little embarrassed, since, once again, there were several other canine patrons at nearby tables. "I know this is presumptuous, but if you're free, could I invite you to dine another night this week? I'd like to introduce you to my daughter." I'm pretty sure she was speaking of me and not JP, but I could never be sure. "Any night, really. I'll hold a table—*la porte est ouverte*. The door is open."

QUEL BORDEL !

"Never, ever? *Même pas une fois* ?" Bonbon asked incredulously. "When Dominique phoned I thought he was talking about you!" The mayor had expressed the same disbelief when I had admitted over dessert that JP was still a virgin—only he had said that JP would instinctively know what to do when the time came. Bonbon wasn't as convinced, and she showed up at the mill first thing in the morning with coffee and a plan.

"I'd like to take you and JP to Marseille today," she said. "We can have a nice lunch somewhere."

"I'd love to—I've never been to Marseille," I said.

"Never?" she asked, shaking her head. "The two of you are so unspoiled!"

• • •

Bonbon made sure that my forest work ended by late morning, when she arrived with a pitcher of water and *citron pressé*. "That's enough for today. You'll dehydrate yourself!" She looked around for JP, who had been exploring while I was working.

"He's just wandering around," I said.

"Not too far, I hope," she said, anxious. She called out to him. "*JP ! Viens nous voir !*"

He came tearing out of the woods in a flash, to Bonbon's delight.

"One of his sisters was a wanderer," she said, reminiscing. "She was one of the girls I was going to keep, but she kept leaving, sometimes going as far as up to La Garde-Freinet or down to Grimaud. That little girl just could not sit still."

Bonbon told me how a traveling salesman had come to see the puppies, hoping to adopt a female. One of the girls had seemed to like the man, but Bonbon had rejected him because of his unstable profession. One day when Bonbon was looking for the telephone number of the *fromager* in town, whom little seven-month-old Julie would often visit, she came across the salesman's card, and she knew she had made a mistake: Julie was born to roam the country.

"It's all as it's meant to be, and there's not anything you or I can do about it. Try as we might, we can only hinder fate for so long," she said. "Julie was his match. And when it comes to who we end up with in this life, we don't have a choice in the matter."

"That is exactly why you don't have to worry about JP wandering," I explained to her: "He'd never leave us." Of course this was true, and she beamed because I had said *us*.

"Now go and get cleaned up," she told me. "A dip in the stream wouldn't hurt Casanova, either," she said of JP, with a coy smile.

•   •   •

By eleven Bonbon and I were en route to Marseille in her semiconvertible *deux-chevaux*. I was happy to have four-wheeled transportation for a change. JP, in the front seat, seemed to miss the fresh air and stood nearly the entire way with his head stuck out through the open roof, except for the occasional movement back inside to lick Bonbon's face. Madame sped along the narrow, winding two-lane Route de la Mole toward Toulon, passing every car that didn't have Var license plates, the drivers of which she assumed would not know how to maneuver their vehicles on these roads, thereby presenting a health risk to us. As beautiful as the first part of the drive was, with its vineyards and forests of oak and aromatic pine trees, my stomach was grateful for the transition to the unattractive citified highways of Toulon.

"*Je suis navrée*," Bonbon said, seeing that even JP was looking a little peaked. "I'm awfully sorry about the rush, but JP has an appointment at half past one, and we shouldn't be late in case they've got other dogs scheduled."

"What appointment?" I asked.

"Just to make sure everything is in order," she said. "Flirt is coming all the way from Britain, after all!"

"You mean we're going to Marseille to see a vet?" I was irked we were going to such trouble for, in my opinion, no good reason, and that she hadn't bothered to tell me. When she'd asked me to bring JP's papers with us, I thought she was just being paranoid in case we were in an accident. "Dominique seems competent to me," I said.

"Gregory, it's not a medical test the boy requires," she said, fixing her JP-smudged eyeliner in the rearview mirror. "It's an instruction in the ways of women!" She caught my perplexed eye in the backseat and added, "Maybe we should arrange a visit next door for you."

• • •

Thankfully for me, the bordello next door had been shut down by the health authorities during a recent raid. Because "Quel Bordel !" was technically licensed as a veterinary clinic, Bonbon explained, it couldn't be shut down. "Not until the creature who runs it croaks, anyway."

In fact, Quel Bordel ! was now the only business on this side road in a crumbling residential area on the outskirts of the red-light district of Marseille. In the window was a female boxer with a red bow around her neck and webbed stockings on her legs.

"You see why I didn't say anything?" Bonbon said, pleased with herself for surprising me. "You've got to see it to believe it. And just wait, you haven't seen *la créature*."

Seated behind a reception desk was "the creature," a thin, catlike woman of about sixty, heavily made up, and certainly looking the part of a madame, but who, when she spoke, sounded as educated as any of my professors from La Sorbonne.

"*Bonjour, bonjour !*" she said. "Could I just have a look at his papers, please? We make sure our girls stay healthy." She opened JP's Carnet de Santé, his French passport containing his health records, and flipped through the pages. "*Très bien, parfait.* He's had all his shots. Does he have any preference? Male? Female?

Breed? In females, today we have Lily," she said, indicating the boxer, whom JP had already sniffed and was completely ignoring. "And a Wheaten terrier and a *dogue*."

I really couldn't believe my eyes or my ears, and I wondered if JP would even be willing to remain there without me — although he did seem to be very anxious to get to who- or whatever was behind a shiny red curtain opposite him.

"Actually, we don't know," Madame said. "It's his first time."

"*Il n'y a aucun problème*," the creature replied. "No problem at all. Definitely the *dogue* for him, then. I think Lily is a bit too passive for this *portrait de virilité* . . . but Mabeline ought to give him a run for your money. *A ce propos*, that will be forty-five euros."

•　•　•

"Give him a double, whatever it is," Bonbon said to the baron, a tall, elegant, heavyset man of Bonbon's age who had probably once been handsome, after he'd asked me what his sommelier could bring me in the way of an aperitif. She grabbed my hand and held it up for the baron to see. "Look at him. He's a nervous wreck. His *compagnon* is *chez* Quel Bordel !" She declined an aperitif for herself because she was driving.

My hand wasn't trembling, but I was anxious about what JP might be feeling and what might transpire between him and other male dogs in the presence of bitches. I wasn't in the habit of leaving him in anyone's charge, never mind a madame's. "A gin and tonic, please," I said.

The baron nodded to his sommelier, patted me on the shoulder, and laughed. "Now what do you suppose there is to be worried about?" he asked.

"I don't know—disease maybe? I never saw *her* dog's papers," I said. "Or a dogfight?"

He shook his head. "Madame Bleue runs an extremely clean and well-monitored establishment. It's really a noble thing she does: All the *chiennes* there are rescued from an otherwise horrible existence at the shelter, and I daresay they're quite fulfilled now! And all the *chiens* are neutered." He winked at Bonbon. "I've been bringing Chester twice a year, spring and autumn, since he was two. I don't intend to breed him, but I've no intention, either, of allowing him to suffer the frustrations of mating seasons and denying him his natural urges. Why, you might as well castrate a dog as do that!" The baron excused himself to greet a glamorous couple arriving with a whippet.

"And you thought *I* was eccentric," Bonbon said. I had never said that, so I knew she thought herself so.

"You know, Gregory, it's not really so risqué," she went on, almost shyly, and then stopped as a waiter arrived with my gin and tonic. She continued speaking only once he had left.

"The dogs don't actually go *all* the way. The females are either just barely going into heat, or just out of it, so the scent is there—and they're sprayed with some sort of *parfum hormonal*—but the dogs won't copulate. There is some very animated play, but it's more like an afternoon of companionship. It also raises the levels of testosterone, which will be very helpful."

The baron caught Bonbon's eye from across the room, and he smiled at her.

"He has a crush on you, Bonbon," I said.

"Oh!" She waved that suggestion away, but not convincingly.

The baron ran his family's Bandol wine-producing château and private adjoining restaurant. Bonbon admitted that they had "courted" when she was a young girl, but she had always been skeptical of their future.

"Call it a woman's instinct," she said. "I didn't think he'd be able to curb his appetite. And I was right—he has *still* never committed to one person."

"So he never married?" I asked.

"Of course he *married*. Who ever heard of a single baron?"

As I tasted one of two incredible reds the baron personally brought to the table, I looked around at the luxury of the room—art, tapestries, antiques, gold and silver chalices—and asked if the fully staffed restaurant was usually more crowded. Ours and the other party's table were the only ones occupied.

"I've never actually seen another person here, either at the vineyard or the restaurant," Bonbon said. "But it doesn't matter—the extent of his wealth is almost *vulgaire*."

"But why does he keep it open, if no one comes?"

"What a strange question," she replied. "You don't choose your vocation, it chooses you. Especially not if you inherit it; it's in the blood. Some people make money at theirs, others don't. And besides, if you've already got money, what better thing to do with it than have a *divin* restaurant at your disposal, right in your own home, anytime you need it? Especially someone like the baron who has a sweet tooth *and* a sour one." She tasted her basil-and pine-nut-encrusted *filet de loup,* and when her mouth was finally empty of savoring it, said, "And it *is divin,* isn't it?"

•   •   •

"You'll send me the bill, Baron?" Bonbon asked, knowing, she later told me, that he never would.

"*Bien sûr,* of course," he said. "Along with a case of the nineteen-ninety-nine, but I do have a favor to ask you, my little Bonbon."

"Oh no. What?"

He looked at her tenderly and I understood that they had once been intimate, and that he had been the one to nickname her *Candy.*

"I'd like one of the offspring this time. And I won't take no for an answer," he said.

"But the litter will be in Britain," she said.

"Just a hop, skip, and a jump over there some weekend." He winked.

•   •   •

"Here's your money. Satisfaction is always guaranteed *chez moi,*" Madame Bleue said, handing Bonbon forty-five euros. When we arrived, JP was sitting in the window where the boxer had been, pouting.

"You could come back another day, but I don't think it will matter. He took a tour of the *maison*, but as soon as he realized you were gone he went straight to that window and he's been staring out of it ever since. Some dogs just aren't very *performant*."

Bonbon was obviously distraught, but defended JP. "I seriously doubt the problem is *chez* JP . . . it's probably the timing and the *disposition* of the *chiennes*," she said indignantly.

Madame Bleue made more of an effort than Bonbon not to take offense. "Possibly, Madame, which is why I am refunding your money," she said without any particular intonation.

UNSTILL WATERS

"ONE REALLY MUST draw the line somewhere," Père shouted into my ear as we sailed through the hills on the scooter. "No one appreciates unconventional behavior more than I do, but really, Bonbon can be positively ridiculous." I had to agree, but it didn't change the fact that JP didn't seem to like other dogs all that much. "Like all of us, dogs have their own personalities, and as an excellent judge of character, I'd say that you have a tendency to be a bit of a loner yourself, *n'est-ce pas ?*"

I nodded.

"Well then!" he shouted.

He thought that the bordello idea had been not only absurd but *absolument criminel*, and he felt sorry that JP had been put through it.

That morning, Père had come looking for us in the forest. JP, during his wanderings the day before, had decided to help me with the *débroussaillage* by pulling shrubs out by their roots, and so I was replanting rather than cutting back. I felt I had to repair the damage quickly: Bonbon had discovered it upon our return from Marseille—and the *échec*, as she referred to the failure at the bordello, had already left her in a dismal mood. I really had wanted to get away, to leave Bonbon free to decide if she wanted to go forward with the breeding, since it seemed possible that JP might not be the procreator she'd hoped for.

Père had brought lunch, and had insisted that the three of us ride on the Vespa to take full advantage of the sea air.

"There's no other water like it!" Père was speaking of Escalet, an isolated cove in Ramatuelle, on the other side of

Saint-Tropez. "A refreshing dip in the Mediterranean will do you both good."

He continued to talk all the way to the beach. I learned that he had taken an early retirement from *l'Eglise* when he was to be transferred from Grimaud to a town at the northern edge of the Var.

"As far as I'm concerned, anywhere in the *arrière pays*, the back country north of Lorgues, isn't really the Var," he said. "I have devoted my life to God and to the people of the Var, not to the politics of the bishop." So he had become the chaplain of a private estate, in a *forêt domaniale* in the hills above *le domaine Clix* that allowed him to practice his vocation—and afforded him an enviable lifestyle. The *châtelain* and his wife were not demanding, requiring his presence only for one or two Masses a week and the occasional baptism or marriage, and so, to his parishioners—whom he still counseled privately—it was as if he had never left the parish.

"And you certainly don't find anything like *that* in the *arrière pays*," Père said when we reached the heights of Ramatuelle, with its rolling hills of *pins parasols*, umbrella pines, and vineyards stretching to the crystal-clear, turquoise waters of the Côte Varoise. I didn't imagine anything that spectacular was found anywhere else in world.

•   •   •

"*Bonjour, mon Père ! Bonjour, Père Cyril !*" cried a young couple who sat up from sunbathing on a smooth, flat boulder a few feet above sea level in a cove with a small sandy beach. "*Pardonnez-nous*, we didn't think you were coming today," the woman said as she gathered their things.

"*Je vous en prie*," Père said, forgiving them, "*et merci*. Sweet couple," he added to me. "They're friends of the *châtelain*. I married them a few years back." Being a private chaplain apparently afforded him his own private sunbathing rock on the French Riviera as well.

A few anchored sailboats dotted the bay, and people walked on the rocks above us, but otherwise we were alone. JP and I swam for about an hour before Père called us in for *thé*. JP was enjoying himself so much in the water that he almost didn't come in, not even after Père had said, "JP, I've got some cheese for *toi, aussi*." In fact, I had never known JP to stay in the water so long, or to swim such distances. He was particularly interested, for some reason, in one of the smaller boats far from us, the only black one, with a *Luxembourgeois* flag. I had to repeatedly call him back when he would paddle in that direction.

Père had brought fruit, cheese, and warm tea in a thermos, all of which he laid out on a very intricately woven and expensive-looking Florentine throw that he had inherited from an Italian widow from La Garde-Freinet. JP was rambunctious, and I had to twist his paw to get him to eat the cheese.

"No doubt he's ill from his misadventure yesterday," Père said.

JP didn't seem ill, just very anxious, and I coaxed him to

relax: "*On se calme, on se calme.*" He sighed and lay down on the cloth, looking very unhappy. "Go back in the water then, if you want," I said. "But stay close."

JP raced to the edge of the rock and dived into the water. He swam close to us at first, keeping an eye on me to see that I was still keeping an eye on him, but he was looking mischievous.

"Don't go out there," I said. He swam to the sandy part of the beach where he could wade and found a piece of driftwood to preoccupy himself with while Père and I finished the *déjeuner.*

I asked Père about Monsieur Clix, whom Bonbon had rarely mentioned. The Clixes had always kept to themselves, Père said, and he had only met Chou-Chou a few times, at local events when everyone's presence was *tout à fait obligatoire,* such as the wedding of the mayor, or Père's own *jubilé,* the celebration of his twentieth year of priesthood. Chou-Chou was small, and not *un*-handsome, Père said, unlike Bonbon whom he told me was really the *belle du bal.*

"They were *très amoureux,*" Père said. "In fact, that's how Bonbon and I became close. Naturally, the funeral was held at the church, and I saw immediately that a person capable of such a profound love was the kind of person I cared to have as a friend.

"Of course," he clarified, "she's still as mad as a hatter and she can't be tolerated for more than a few hours at a time. *Franchement,* I don't know how you do it."

. . .

"Would you do something about your dog!" A man's voice shouted from afar, breaking into our conversation. Père and I could barely make out the figure of JP on the deck of the black boat. The boat's owner was using something that looked like an oar or a broom to ward JP off.

"Do something!" Père said to me. "Don't you dare harm that dog!" he shouted to the man.

I swam out to the boat as fast as I could, some two hundred yards at least. I was panting, and not much use physically, by the time I reached it.

"What aphrodisiac is he on, anyway?" the man said. "Call him off!"

JP was not being aggressive, but I saw what was exciting him: Behind the man, trembling in fear and softly whimpering, was a Weimaraner. JP was drooling and panting, and he would not look at me.

"JP, get over here," I said, angrily. He backed up a few inches in my direction but still did not look at me, only at the dog. "Did he hurt him?" I asked.

"*Her*," the man corrected. "Not yet, he didn't, but she's in heat."

I didn't bother to hide my contentment that JP *could* be *performant* if he wanted to.

"I'm glad you find it amusing, but Daphné is only a nine-month old puppy. Now please climb up that ladder and remove the monster from my boat."

JP didn't resist once I was on board. I lifted him up and threw him overboard, apologizing to the man.

"Oh, *ça va quoi*, it's okay," he shrugged, mellow now that Daphné was safely wrapped in his arms. "She's irresistible, my girl. But you might want to keep a *prédateur* like that on a leash—she's been around males before, but none quite so assertive."

"I agree—and again, I'm sorry," I said, overjoyed and anxious to tell Bonbon the good news.

The good news would have to wait a bit longer. Both my legs cramped up halfway back to shore, with a hundred feet still to go. I could only use my arms to keep my head above water, and when my speed slowed, JP knew something was wrong. He decelerated himself and treaded water around me, blocking me. "JP get away—just go to shore, please," I managed to get out, my head bobbing in and out of the water. He began to howl.

"Gray-goh-ree? Greg? Is everything . . . ," I heard Père shout before my head went under.

I knew that, above all, I shouldn't panic, but I could see that I was at least a foot beneath the surface and did not have the strength to swim to shore and keep my head up—and it was hard not to. I couldn't hold my breath any longer and was trying not to think about the water I was taking into my mouth, and how it should feel like I was choking on it but didn't, and how that was probably bad.

JP sank deeper into the water, clawing at me, coming at me from all sides, trying to pull at my shorts—he was panicked, too, and that was only making things worse. I pushed him away, and when he spun around I grabbed his hips. He stopped struggling, giving me the time to clamp my hands around his stomach. Instantly his legs started pumping hard, with a backlash against my stomach as he struggled with the extra weight, and I marveled at his strength.

When we emerged from the water, Père stood on the rock, mesmerized. "There *is* a God," he said.

•   •   •

"As God is my witness, it's true, all of it!" Père exclaimed.

Bonbon really wanted to believe it, but it sounded too good to be true. "It's all right if it's not true—I've already come to accept the inevitable, if that's how it must be," she said, meaning that JP might be impotent.

Père interjected, scoldingly: "I don't care what *condition* those *chiennes* are in, or what kind of *parfums* they might be sprayed with, any hot-blooded *chien* knows when a *chienne* is in heat or not! And I want you to promise me you'll never set foot in a place of such ill repute ever again."

Bonbon lowered her head and seemed to be on the verge of apologizing, but not quite. "Do you swear, both of you?" she asked quietly.

This time I interjected. "You're really quite disrespectful and rude, Bonbon," I said. She looked at me in mock horror. "I mean, it's disrespectful to imply that a priest is telling an untruth . . . and rude to suggest that JP is anything less than a stud."

Bonbon lit up like the lightbulb she had been switching on and off all day.

THE BUTCHER

"Not the Italian one! I'd have loved that myself," Bonbon said the next morning, when I recounted the latter part of the adventures at Escalet Beach that we had spared her: including how, while Père was watching our toil back to shore, a band of Gypsies had managed to make off with his throw. We saw them running with it, but they were too far off.

"At least the straw basket was still there," I said.

"Hmmph," Bonbon said, looking bemused. "Strange they didn't take that."

"Luckily. My keys and Père's wallet were in it."

"It was handmade as well," she said, offended. "I bought that for him at the Saint-Tropez market."

●   ●   ●

JP and I spent the morning finishing the *débroussaillage*. It had become more than a chore and less of an inconvenience. In fact, I began to look forward more to that task than to my morning coffee when I woke each day, and now that I could see the fruits of my labor, I felt like I had really accomplished something. I had never worked the land before, despite the fact that it is such a part of the French way of life. No matter what their profession, the French take the time to be a part of the land they borrow, not only because they feel they are one with nature, but also to nurture and protect it, so that it is rich and healthy for the next generation.

"It's not my forest. I'm just passing through," Bonbon would say, even though she did by default refer to everything living or inanimate at *le domaine Clix* as hers.

•   •   •

Clearing out the forest had also revealed a fenced-in garden in the center of the forest that I hadn't noticed. At lunch I asked Bonbon about it.

"You've discovered our Cabbage Patch," she said, and I knew it had some special meaning to her: She never called anything *our*, and it dawned on me that the translation of *chou*, the word making up her late husband's double-barreled nickname of *Chou-Chou*, was "cabbage." "You'll see it soon enough," she told me, and I decided not to press her, because she had said that she could not stomach green and leafy vegetables.

"I suppose you'll be going into the village today." She said this as if it were a wicked thing to do but there would be no stopping me.

"Not necessarily," I said, teasing, because of course I was. "Did you need something?"

"Only if you're already planning to go in."

"What is it?"

"Steaks," she said. "Fresh ones. *Figurez-vous*, that's all Flirt eats, they told me . . . and probably all the Englishman and his wife will want as well," she added disdainfully, as if rare steak were not the main ingredient of her own diet. "And I suppose I've no choice but to have them for dinner at least once." She handed me a list of cuts to order.

"I can go in any day," I said. "Shouldn't we wait until they arrive so it will be fresh?"

"Only if you want to go at dawn. They're arriving tomorrow morning. JP's big day is near."

·　　·　　·

"How dare you!" Madame Poulin said as JP and I scooted past her house.

"*Bonjour* Madame Poulin," I called out.

"How dare you!" she repeated, and I knew I'd better turn around.

"How dare I what?" I asked, parking the Vespa in her walkway.

"Set foot in this village without saying hello. I told you the door was always open." JP took her at her word and strode past her and through the door.

"*Mes amours,*" she said to us when we were both safely inside. "*Vraiment,* I have told everyone who'll listen about the wonderful flowers *le jeune américain* brought me. The other *filles* are very *jalouses.*" She winked. "Don't worry, I've told them that I won't monopolize you—and that I'll even baby-sit for JP if any one of them manages to get a date with you."

"You're just using me for my dog," I told her.

"Hauh! If you knew how many times I've been passed over for a dog!" She gave JP a piece of Swiss cheese.

"Madame Poulin, do you know where can I find the butcher?" I asked.

"Which one?"

"The best one."

"Aren't we *chic*," she said. "If you want to pay the most, go to the one in the village. If you want the freshest meat, go down to the plain." The plain was the flat farmland at the foot of the village. She tore a piece of paper from a pad and drew me a map. "He's got a screw loose, that one, but he's got the best meat around. Take it from a *paysanne*." She held out the map and another piece of cheese. "And don't forget, *la porte est grande ouverte !* The door is *wide* open!"

· · ·

The door to the butcher was not wide open, however, and JP and I waited fifteen minutes before a car pulled up and a woman got out.

"Sorry," she said insincerely, "Didier is sleeping. It *is* Sunday, after all." JP, who had gone around to the back of the farm to sniff things out, reappeared. "Well look at you," she said, in a slightly warmer tone.

"You wouldn't be able to help me in Didier's absence, would you?" I asked.

"Only if you're with a restaurant," she said, and glanced at her watch.

"I'm not."

"It's Sunday, and it's after noon." She shrugged. It was exactly noon.

"I've been here since quarter till," I told her.

"Impossible." JP rubbed himself against her leg, and she reached down to pet him. "Well look at you," she said again to him, and then to me, "Well, *exceptionnellement*. Just this once."

Inside, she opened up a glass case of the freshest meat I had ever seen, aside from the chicken livers in Yvelines. It was still dripping with blood. "When did you, ahm . . . ," I started.

"Butcher this?" she offered. I nodded. "Well we don't do it ourselves, if that's what you mean, but"—she looked at her watch—"probably going on six hours ago, maybe seven." I handed her the list, and she started chopping away with various knives for the different cuts.

"*Voilà*," she said, when she had finished. And then, "No, wait." She took what looked to me to be a very prime cut and threw it to JP, and he sat down at her feet and began to eat it. "Well look at you," she said. I took out my wallet and she told me that it would cost "about" sixty euros. I wondered how much more expensive the village butcher could have been. Luckily I had some more cash in my saddle bag and went to get it.

When I returned, the butcher's wife was on her knees beside JP, whispering sweet nothings to him, about how handsome he was, and how there would be more meat for him when he was done with that. I put sixty euros on the counter and she said, "Make it fifty."

Suddenly a door was thrown open and the meat man from the *marché* whose *saucisson* I had rejected, stormed in, cursing, waving a very large cleaver at me.

"Who the hell are you giving discounts to!" he shouted.

"I was talking to the dog, you idiot," his wife said. "Now put that down."

The man grew even more enraged. "I'll put it down all right—on his head!" He came toward me, red-faced. His wife walked out of the room. JP jumped in front of me and, for the first time in his life, started growling.

"What is going on in here!" In jeans and a black leather jacket, Madame Girard looked more like a sexy Hell's Angels chick than a fashionable *restauratrice*. "Put that thing down, Didier. Now," she said.

"No! I won't! Not until he apologizes for coming on to my wife, until he *begs* me to put it down."

Madame Girard let her shoulder bag slide down to the ground. "Didier," she said, "No man in his right mind would ever be interested in your ugly wife, and if you don't put that thing down, *I'll* use *this* one." She picked up a normal-sized knife lying on the counter. "And I'll turn you into tonight's main course."

There was a tense moment when I thought she might actually carry out her threat, but Didier gave in and dropped the cleaver—which turned out to be rubber, although his rage was definitely not faked.

"Are you all right?" Madame Girard asked. "He really ought to be committed. I'm going straight to the police."

"Yvonne, please don't," Didier said, tears welling up in his eyes. "I just love her so much, and everybody wants her. One day she'll leave me. I know it." He moved toward her as if to hug her, or apologize, or something, but JP would not let him approach.

"*Tu as raison, JP*," she said. "Keep away from me, Didier, if you know what's good for you."

"Just take whatever you need, it's yours," Didier said, and walked out.

Madame Girard shrugged. She looked at the money on the counter. "Is that yours?" she asked. I nodded. She picked it up and put it in my hand. "His whole family is crazy. He ought to be put away—or at least not be left around knives—I think it's the meat and blood that gets to him."

She went behind the counter and took stock of what was on offer. "*Monsieur—*" she started.

"Greg," I said.

"—Gregory," she completed. "And it's Yvonne *pour moi*. If you haven't lost your appetite, why don't you and JP come to dinner tonight?" She lifted up legs of this and breasts of that. "My daughter is home from university. She's dying to meet him." She pulled out a leg of lamb and tossed it to JP.

It was hard to believe she could have a college-aged daughter. I told her I felt like *I* should be taking *her* to dinner, for saving my life.

"Saving it from what, *that?*" She laughed at the rubber thing lying on the ground. "No." She motioned outside, in the direction of the scooter. "But you can take me for a ride on that Vespa sometime."

"Anytime."

"*Je plaisante*, I've got bad knees from an accident. I can hardly bend them anymore. But I miss riding. I used to have a Harley. Anyway, it's up to you about dinner. I'll have a nice corner table for you, with some room for JP to move around. If you come, you come, if you don't, you don't."

She spun a large roll of brown paper, cut a piece off, and plopped the choicest cuts she had selected for herself. She looked up at me and smiled. I put my money back into my wallet. "It's the least he can do for us," she said, conspiratorially. "Don't you agree?" I did. And I also thought Yvonne was the most bewitching woman I'd ever met.

•   •   •

"What!" Bonbon practically screamed. "Why didn't you go to the butcher in the village?"

"Someone told me he was the one to go to," I said.

"Yes, for a freak show! It must run in the family. That man's father killed my ass. He used to be our *gardien* and when we sacked him, he shot our ass! Shot him dead! He denied it, but I know it was him!" She paced around the room, with JP following her every step, his attempt at comforting her. It seemed to work.

When she had calmed down enough to hear me, I said, "Yes, the whole family is crazy. I wish I had known."

She sat down. "It's not your fault. You couldn't have known."

"I walked out of there without paying, if it's any consolation." It was, and she smiled. And so were the flowers I had bought for her, and this time actually delivered.

$$\bullet \quad \bullet \quad \bullet$$

"Stéphanie, is he a cutie, or what?" Yvonne asked her twenty-one-year-old daughter, who had inherited Yvonne's looks, but not her intensity.

"Yes, I want one!" Stéphanie said. For a split second that I didn't manage to conceal, I thought they meant me, but of course they didn't.

"JP, this thing with you is getting serious," I said. "Your job is to get *me* noticed." JP tilted his head and looked at me sideways, questioning, wanting only to please me.

Yvonne laughed, raspy, deep, and contagious. "You managed to get yourself noticed by Didier's wife today," she said.

"No." I shook my head. "Even that was because of JP."

"No," she said, thinking I was joking, and then, "Really?" I nodded and she burst out laughing. "Wait until I tell the chef!"

•   •   •

The chef was a pudgy, jolly man whom at first I never would have believed could be Yvonne's husband. He joined JP and me at our corner table, strategically placed so that JP could have a French windowsill balcony to walk onto for air. Monsieur Girard wanted to hear the tale from the horse's mouth, he said, since Yvonne was prone to exaggeration.

While I told the story, the chef hid his hands under the table so that JP could lick the traces of the *délices de Provence* he'd been preparing. "Yes, that sounds like Didier. And *exactly* like Yvonne." He stood up and walked back to the kitchen, barreling out a hearty laugh that came from somewhere deep and soulful, and I understood why they were together, and how they had built such a wonderful place as Les Santons.

•   •   •

"*Parfait*," Père said as Stéphanie seated him at the one remaining table—in the opposite corner—at a little after ten. When JP heard Père's voice, he couldn't resist: He got up, walked over to Père, and climbed into his lap. "My goodness, JP, I'm all in black!" he said. JP got off, but only reluctantly.

Yvonne walked over to Père, laughing, and double-air-kissed him. "You always wear black. Nothing is wrong with gray," she said. With the dozens of JP's hairs now glued to Père's jacket, it did look gray in the light of the candles.

"But it's my nice jacket," he said, scolding JP.

"All your jackets are nice," Yvonne said.

"Thank you," Père said, without a hint of modesty.

"You know *Monsieur l'Abbé*, too?" Yvonne asked me.

"Oh yes!" Père answered for me. "I've even been on the Vespa!"

"That's more than I've had!" Yvonne glared mock-angrily at me for a moment, and then smiled. "But we have to be nice to Gregory. He's lucky to be here at all."

"And why is that?"

"He was nearly killed today."

Père shook his head, looking as if he were about to pray for my soul—but ready to hear a good story.

THE CABBAGE PATCH

"Madame, the coupling will not take place in the woods," Mr. Wilkes-Boggs said in English, and looked around. "Now, what sort of enclosed spaces do you have on the property?"

Bonbon would not look at Mr. Wilkes-Boggs. "What is he saying?"

I translated.

"*Non*," she said simply.

"No, *what?*" Mr. Wilkes-Boggs said.

"Tell him that the *mariage* will take place in the Cabbage Patch, or not at all," Bonbon said.

Mr. Wilkes-Boggs looked at his wife and said, "Did she say *marriage?* Is that what she thinks this is?"

"Apparently so," Mrs. Wilkes-Boggs said, inclining her head in the direction of Père, who was hurrying over.

"So how are things going with the two lovebirds?" Père asked in English, provocatively.

"Hello," Mr. Wilkes-Boggs said, ignoring the question.

Bonbon was determined that the union between JP and Flirt would take place in the Cabbage Patch, and that they wouldn't be restrained by leashes; and Mr. Wilkes-Boggs was just as adamant that Flirt be in an enclosed area so that she couldn't try to flee. If she did so when the dogs were "tied" during the final stage of copulation, it could cause serious harm to her.

"None of *my* dogs has ever attempted to break a tie," Bonbon said. "Surely you can't expect Flirt to be *held* for the entire time—it could take thirty minutes." I'd seen photographs of breeding dogs stuck together, back to back, virtually inseparable, but I had no idea that it could last for half an hour.

Père saw the look on my face. "Dreadful, isn't it," he said.

"Oh it isn't *dreadful,* it's *normal!*" Bonbon said.

Bonbon asked me to instruct the Wilkes-Boggses to return in the afternoon, by which time the Cabbage Patch would be an *enclos* for JP and Flirt.

•   •   •

"I won't be insulted and affronted," Bonbon said. She was annoyed by Mr. Wilkes-Boggs's dismissal of her romantic ideas about how and where dogs should couple.

"Or ridiculed and mocked," I added, trying to make light of it.

"*Really* Bonbon," Père said. "Why can't they just do it in the *garage* and be done with it?" The three of us were working to patch a six-foot-wide gap in the fence surrounding the Cabbage Patch to conciliate Mr. Wilkes-Boggs—it was hot, and Père was growing *fatigué.*

Bonbon pretended to look horrified. "I never in a million years would have believed that you two could gang up on me," she said, holding a piece of plastic sheeting over Père's head menacingly. She looked at JP, who was standing between Père and me—on our side, as it were—tilting his head and looking at Bonbon questioningly. "You *three!*" She laughed.

My relationship with Bonbon had transcended another barrier

now that we regularly teased each other, and that, in turn, was transforming the relationship between Bonbon and Père into something less prescribed. Whereas before Bonbon would shake Père's hand when greeting him, she now air-kissed him, and occasionally even squeezed his arm or shoulder. And Père, who had always phoned to make an appointment with Bonbon, would now show up unannounced, as if he were an extended member of her family.

Indeed, pounding a stake into the ground with the blunt end of an ax was an enterprise Père had never undertaken with a parishioner. The sight of him, in black priest's garb complete with collar tab, a paste of sweat and dust on his forehead, brought Bonbon and me to uncontrollable laughter.

"If anything good has come of this latest American and British invasion, it's that it has prompted *Monsieur l'Abbé* to lift his first finger and break his first sweat!" Bonbon said.

Père came after her with the ax and Bonbon screamed. JP, ever the serious one, stood back, observing us all, not knowing which side to take now, thinking we had all gone mad—and reminding us of the exigency of the task at hand.

Père and Bonbon held the two ends of the plastic sheet while I commenced the painstakingly slow process of sawing it down the middle. Bonbon occasionally lost her grip, her mind wandering.

"Chou-Chou wasn't much of a talker," she said suddenly.

"I shouldn't imagine he'd have been able to get a word in edgewise," Père said.

"*Touché !*" Bonbon said, but she was lost in her memories, and soon Père and I were as well, as she recounted them.

"He and I used to spend hours just sitting here, listening to the *cigales*, the summer cicadas, and not say a word to each other, not a single word," Bonbon said. It *was* hard to imagine her silent, and before Père could make that observation, she said, "Yes, I *am* capable of prolonged silence. I think that's why Chou-Chou and I got along so well . . . we hardly ever spoke. We never needed to."

Bonbon was thirty-four when she met Chou-Chou, *né* Bernard, by what she thought was chance at a family gathering she'd been loath to attend. Both of their families were in shipping, members of Marseille's elite set, and both of them had already escaped that world for a more exciting *existence* in Paris where their paths had never crossed, "perhaps by design, even," Bonbon said, "so determined were we to sever ties with the *culture marseillaise*. But that's all either of us was doing in Paris, really, merely *existing*."

Bored, Bonbon had left the yacht party and walked to the edge of a pier to smoke. A man was sitting there with his legs dangling off the pier.

"Do you mind?" he'd said.

"Not at all," Bonbon answered, thinking he wanted to be alone. She walked to the other side of the pier to light her cigarette, when the man swooped up behind her and blew out the flame of her gold *briquet*.

"I mean the cigarette," he'd said, with his hand cupped over hers. "It's so unpleasant to embrace a lady with tobacco breath."

"And there I thought I was so smart with my Cartier lighter and my Parisian ways," Bonbon said, reflecting. "I never lit another cigarette again, and for the first time in years, I felt alive, just being next to him.

"The two people I had always resented most in my life were to thank for Chou-Chou," Bonbon continued. One was the baron for freeing her heart, she only just admitted then; and the other was her mother, who had always tried to control Bonbon, and who had arranged for Bernard to meet her that night.

"The Cabbage Patch was Chou-Chou's very first endeavor to harvest something from the land, and he chose it simply because he liked the stuff!" Bonbon mused. "No one else grew cabbage in the Var. For one thing, it's not the right soil."

But Bernard knew that the best way to have a fruitful harvest was by cultivating what you loved. Cabbage . . . Bonbon was not overly fond of that particular vegetable, but she was someone who loved love itself, and so she kept up the Cabbage Patch when Bernard died, and it became a place where love could be sown.

"I still scatter a few seeds here and there in his honor, of course, but as you can see, they're not exactly thriving," Bonbon said.

There was a wrought-iron bench, Bernard's, beneath which she had planted his ashes, and around which, it must be said, the healthier of the purple and green cabbage plants grew. When I had finished cutting, Bonbon sat down on the bench and I nailed the panel to Père's lopsided wooden post.

"How does that look?" I asked.

Bonbon was far away. "I was never able to have children," she said.

•   •   •

"Oh God, the vicar is still here," Père and I heard Mr. Wilkes-Boggs say to his wife as he exited his Range Rover. "The old bat *does* think it's a marriage."

"The *vicar* is present merely for moral support on behalf of the *Veuve Clix*," he said mostly in English, as if to imply that Bonbon was still in mourning for Bernard, which I believe she was.

"*Veuve?*" Mr. Wilkes-Boggs asked his wife quietly. "What is that?"

"Widow," I answered gravely.

"Oh! I'm terribly sorry," said Mr. and Mrs. Wilkes-Boggs simultaneously.

"I don't mean to trouble you," Mr. Wilkes-Boggs said to me, "but could you, would you be so kind as to take the dog away while I remove Flirt from the vehicle? If you don't have a lead, I've an extra one."

He handed me a leash, which I attached to JP. He was excitedly scratching at the rear hatch, trying to catch a glimpse of the female behind its tinted windows.

"We'll arrive presently, but it's best if the dog is already in the pen," Mr. Wilkes-Boggs said.

"*On va voir Bonbon*," I said, pulling JP with some difficulty away from the Range Rover, and leading him around to the back of the *manoir* where Bonbon was waiting.

Bonbon, Mrs. Wilkes-Boggs, and I walked JP to the Cabbage Patch while Père remained with Mr. Wilkes-Boggs to be able to show him how to get to the "pen."

Mrs. Wilkes-Boggs made an effort to win Bonbon's affection. "You don't know what it has been like," she said. "The hotel where we've been staying for the past three days—it's lovely, of course, but there are two unneutered males who are clearly desperate to get at Flirt!"

Bonbon stared at her in silence, and then opened the gate to the Cabbage Patch.

"In any case, I'm delighted the moment has finally come," Mrs. Wilkes-Boggs said.

Bonbon walked to the bench and sat down. "What hotel?" she said to me. "I thought they were staying with friends at *La Garde-Anglais*." *La Garde-Anglais* was her rhyming metaphor for La Garde-Freinet, a favorite vacation spots for Brits.

Mrs. Wilkes-Boggs explained that they had decided to stay at the Coteau Fleuri, because of the view and the nice walks behind the village of Grimaud.

"The Coteau Fleuri!" Bonbon cried. "That awful man *hunts* my little boars!" Bonbon also thought of the nocturnal pests that dug holes and uprooted bamboo at *le domaine Clix* as hers. "I imagine I'll receive the bill for the room as well," she muttered.

GREGORY EDMONT

"*Vous y avez dîné ?*" Bonbon wanted to know what they'd eaten—if they had feasted on fresh kills, even though she knew it wasn't hunting season. Mrs. Wilkes-Boggs understood enough to know that she had said something to further offend Bonbon, and she looked at me pleadingly.

"Those hunters," I translated.

"Yes, I'm very much against hunting," Mrs. Wilkes-Boggs agreed.

"*Ah bon,* really?" Bonbon said, consoled slightly.

Mrs. Wilkes-Boggs breathed a sigh of relief. I, too, was relieved: that I'd never thought to mention to Bonbon that I had stayed and dined at the Coteau Fleuri.

"Oh yes," Mrs. Wilkes-Boggs added, to her detriment. "Rupert and I are both vegetarians."

"*Ah bon,*" Bonbon said, rolling her eyes.

Bonbon stood up and took a deep breath when Père and Mr. Wilkes-Boggs arrived at the gate. Mr. Wilkes-Boggs held Flirt, a pretty, petite, and trembling liver-spotted Dalmatian.

"She looks smaller than in the pictures you sent," Bonbon said.

Mr. Wilkes-Boggs looked at me. "She looks just like her pictures," I said.

Bonbon frowned. She had told me how difficult it was to find decent liver bitches in France. Every few years she would fly to England (despite what she may personally think of the English, they did breed fine canine specimens), pick out a female puppy at five to eight weeks of age, and hope that when the puppy was shipped a couple of months later, she would turn out to be of breeding quality. The Wilkes-Boggses had insisted that all of their expenses be covered, since JP, although *confirmé,* was not considered a champion and had never been shown, and there was therefore no guarantee that the litter would be profitable. So while the new method of covering the Wilkes-Boggses' travel expenses was more costly, it was less of a long-term risk for Bonbon. In any case, Bonbon would have the pick of the litter, a new female, to carry on the line.

Now I wondered if, after all this, Bonbon might reject Flirt. As it turned out, she didn't have to.

Once inside the Cabbage Patch, JP and Flirt remained as far away from each other as possible, at diagonally opposing camps, like boxers in a ring, accompanied by their owners. Flirt looked terrified, and JP looked bored—he stretched, yawned, and lay down.

"Come along now, JP," said Mrs. Wilkes-Boggs. "Isn't Flirt pretty!"

"What makes her think it's his fault?" Père said in French. "She's not exactly alluring, shaking like that, contorted into a pile of furry bones."

Mr. Wilkes-Boggs looked again to me for an interpretation of the commentary. "Is Flirt shy?" I said.

"Not at all, she's already whelped twice—two perfectly healthy litters," Mr. Wilkes-Boggs insisted. "Has the *male* ever coupled before?"

"No," I said. A look passed between Mr. and Mrs. Wilkes-Boggs.

"It *can* happen, you know," Mrs. Wilkes-Boggs said. "There is such a thing as a homosexual dog."

"Oh for heaven's sake, Madame," Père said in English.

"It's true," she said. "I was raised with one."

"You probably drove him to it," Père said in French.

Bonbon was sitting on the bench, silent and miserable. I coaxed JP to go to Flirt, and he started to walk toward her. When he got to within a few feet of her she flung her tail to the side. Bonbon stood up, hopeful.

"She's assuming position! Hold her," Mrs. Wilkes-Boggs said to her husband, and the latter held Flirt's leash tightly.

Bonbon rolled her eyes. "They're a bit *névrosés*, neurotic, aren't they?" she said to me. "This business of positions and clutching her is not making it any easier—*enfin, ce n'est pas très romantique*. I mean, really, it's not exactly romantic."

JP sniffed Flirt, interested.

"*Oui, c'est ça, c'est ça*," Bonbon said, encouraging JP.

But suddenly JP stopped, looked at me, licked Mrs. Wilkes-Boggs's hands in their frozen, clapped position, and walked back to his corner, by the gate, staring in the direction of the *manoir*. He began to whine.

Even though Mr. Wilkes-Boggs had studied to be a veterinarian himself, and had had years of breeding experience, he agreed to have Flirt seen by Dominique, just to make certain that her eggs were dropping. But even I knew enough from what I'd read that when a bitch assumed position, it meant she was ready. And I knew JP well enough to know that if he wasn't interested in someone, there was no forcing him. For the first night since my arrival in the country of France, I had no appetite for dinner—and I wondered if I'd be able to afford one, since there would almost surely be no stud fee forthcoming.

LOVE AT FIRST BITE

"TAKE A DEEP breath and spit it out!" Bonbon said, trying to be calm so that I would. I was trying to form the words but couldn't. I had awakened to find the kitchen door wide open, and JP gone. I wanted to say: *Please, Bonbon, do something. I know you can do something.* But the words that came were: "It's your fault!"

Anna María insisted that with the help of Lulu, she and Samuel would be able to find JP. I knew they wouldn't, and so did Bonbon. We couldn't feel his presence. He had left sometime during the night, and I was certain, I told Bonbon, that it was because he had sensed our profound disappointment, our conditional love.

"Gregory," she said, "know that I will not eat, drink, or sleep until JP is found." I started to apologize for what I had blurted out, but she put a finger to my lips. "It *is* my fault. Everything is my fault," she said, and I was heartbroken for her, and sorry for my pathetic self.

The night before Bonbon had come down to the mill to say good night. As soon as I opened the door, as if reading my mind she had said, "No matter what happens, you'll have your fee. These things happen—there's no guarantee. I'm responsible for breeding JP, and I daresay our trip to Marseille may have hindered the process rather than helped it." She had wanted to shoulder the responsibility, and she was sad. JP, too, had been out of sorts, and hadn't even come downstairs when she knocked. "Tomorrow's another day," Bonbon had said, and left.

"Who *cares* whether or not the door was locked, Cyril!" Bonbon shouted, guilty of the same kind of irrational outburst as mine. I think Père was more surprised by hearing his Christian name spoken so nakedly than by the insulting tone.

I said that it was possible that I hadn't locked the door behind Bonbon the night before—I hadn't thought JP capable of leaving.

"This is no time for pedantry, Père," Bonbon said.

"You're right," he said, simply.

"No, I'm not," she said, and hugged him, her way of a graceful apology, which was more than I had been capable of offering her.

By nine o'clock Bonbon had phoned the police department, the fire department, the town hall, and Dominique; no one had seen or heard anything. I knew that JP would not go into traffic, not willingly go with a stranger, and not fight with other dogs, but I didn't know if he would disobey a command to get into a car or if he would be able to defend himself against Bonbon's wild boar who roamed the hills at night.

At ten o'clock the very punctual Wilkes-Boggses arrived. They were upbeat, determined that we'd have better luck today. When Bonbon told them the news, Mrs. Wilkes-Boggs became so upset she was on the verge of tears, and I saw Bonbon warm to her.

"A bitch in heat can do strange things to a dog's chemistry," she said. "It can make them run away. But I'm sure he'll be back. The scent of Flirt may even bring him back."

Mr. Wilkes-Boggs frowned. "Not if he's run away *from* Flirt, darling." Mrs. Wilkes-Boggs shook her head, and her husband stopped speaking.

"Do let the girls out of the Range Rover, Rupert," she said.

This time when Mr. Wilkes-Boggs opened the hatch, one dog jumped out: Flirt, still a bit skittish, but at least not trembling; and another dog *stepped* out behind her, gracefully, with an almost unnerving calm. It wasn't that she was more beautiful than Flirt, but she was taller, younger, leaner, and she had the same kind of presence as JP. I could tell from the way Bonbon was staring at her that she thought the same thing.

"Our other bitch, Marvella of Delaunay," Mrs. Wilkes-Boggs said. "Isn't she lovely?"

•   •   •

It was Père who suggested that we call Madame Poulin — after all, he said, if anyone in the village would hear news first it would be her.

"Yes, he was here for his cheese first thing," she said to me on the phone. "Where in the world are *you?*" I was filled with relief that JP was all right, but I was haunted by Mr. Wilkes-Boggs's words, *run away*, and anguished that JP could ever do it.

"If he comes back, please keep him with you," I said.

"I'll do that, but I expect you'll find him at the Coteau Fleuri. I hear he's been loitering there all morning."

As Anna María prepared a vegetarian lunch for the Wilkes-Boggses, and a roast for Samuel (who was more than happy to relieve Bonbon of the surplus steak, and to practice his English), Bonbon and I drove to the village. Père was exhausted and thought he should wait at *le domaine,* in case JP came home first.

•　　•　　•

"I feel like I'm running a kennel," Mr. Minard said, only half joking. "I've had complaints from Spanish guests for two days straight about all the dogs."

I made excuses for JP, explaining that we had been trying to breed him, that his chemistry must be out of whack, and asked if he was there.

"Last time I saw him, it was before dawn. He was sleeping by the door of the English truck. When I came outside, he left—I think he went up the hill."

I thanked him, and called JP's name a few times, knowing it was futile.

"He'll turn up. They always do," he said. He waved at the *deux-chevaux.* Bonbon saw but pretended she didn't.

Mr. Minard frowned. "Is that Madame Clix in the car?"

"She's been having trouble with her eyes," I fibbed.

"She never seems to recognize me," he said. "Anyway, don't worry about JP. He's certainly got a good nose on him, to come all the way down from your neck of the woods for a bitch in heat. You should try hunting with us sometime."

Bonbon and I combed the village and as much of the surrounding hills as we could. We shouted for JP until our voices were hoarse, but it was hopeless.

. . .

Discouraged, Bonbon and I were having coffee on the terrace with Mr. and Mrs. Wilkes-Boggs while the girls played in the garden next to them.

"Rupert!" Mrs. Wilkes-Boggs suddenly cried. JP was charging out of the woods, and bounding across the garden toward them.

"JP!" I shouted. He wagged his tail wildly at me, but nonetheless made a beeline toward Flirt and Marvella.

"Grab Flirt!" she said.

"*Don't* grab her!" Bonbon said. "For God's sake, let them *be!*"

Mr. Wilkes-Boggs jumped up from the table and first ran toward Flirt, who in turn ran from him, and then tried to no avail to intercept JP.

"He can't take her like this," Mrs. Wilkes-Boggs said.

"I don't know who is worse, really," Bonbon said, "her or me." But her attempt at sarcasm was drowned in her delight at JP's return.

When she got to the edge of the garden, Flirt froze, assumed position, and started trembling.

Now that JP had stopped running, we could see what a really awful state he was in. He had run home several miles through the forest, and he was covered in thorns, bleeding in some spots. Panting and foaming at the mouth, he looked almost rabid.

"My God," Mrs. Wilkes-Boggs said when she got a good look at him. "I don't think we should do this today."

"No, no, it's all right," Mr. Wilkes-Boggs said. "This is just what he needed—to get worked up a bit." For a few seconds, no one moved. JP stood still, panting, trying to catch his breath. I stood on the terrace with Bonbon, who was strangely contemplative, observing JP. The Wilkes-Boggses were squatting, holding and caressing Flirt. Marvella was ignoring everything around her, delicately nibbling the petals of Bonbon's flowers at the edge of the terrace. JP finally advanced, not in Flirt's direction, but in Marvella's.

"No, boy," Mr. Wilkes-Boggs laughed. "Not *that* one. It's this one over here."

JP began to lick one of Marvella's ears, but she did not divert her attention from the flowers. "*JP, là-bas,*" I started to say, indicating Flirt, but Bonbon put her hand on my arm to stop me. I looked at her, and she shook her head silently.

JP licked Marvella's other ear and then her head, repeatedly. Then he began to nuzzle her neck. She stopped nibbling the flowers for a moment, but only to stretch. Growing impatient, JP charged playfully, trying to lure her into a friskier game, but she would have none of it. She lay down on the grass, toying with a stem she had plucked for herself.

JP crouched down next to her and started pawing her, at which point Marvella drew the line: She turned around and nipped him on the leg, just hard enough to let him know that she was not that kind of girl. He yelped as if she had taken a bite out of him, moved a few feet away, lay down, and sulked, all the while never taking his eyes off her.

Flirt barked, demanding that some attention be paid to her.

JP glanced only briefly in her direction to see if there was anything to it; there wasn't. His focus was again on Marvella, and he began to emit a low-pitched hum, somewhere between a whine and a growl, to let her know how hurt he was. Marvella stopped chewing her stem, and for a few moments the two dogs stared at each other. JP ceased the noise he was making, perked up his ears, and waited, transfixed and hopeful.

Marvella got up and slowly, daintily, walked to JP. She let the stem fall from her mouth to the ground at the tip of JP's nose. JP didn't take it, and only continued to watch her. Marvella lowered her head and licked JP on the nose. He lifted his head, and they gave each other a mutual lick. JP's tail began to wag frantically; Marvella, too, allowed her tail to wag, just once back and forth. She then lay down beside JP, her body touching his, and the two of them fell sound asleep. Flirt barked again, but with less resolve, and this time JP didn't hear it.

"This is madness," Mr. Wilkes-Boggs said.

"No," Bonbon said quietly, shaking her head. "This is love."

Mr. Wilkes-Boggs looked at her as if she were out of her mind, but I could tell that Mrs. Wilkes-Boggs wasn't so sure. And I knew that Bonbon was right; that when it comes to whom we end up with in this life, we don't have a choice in the matter. It's all as it's meant to be, and there's not anything anyone can do about it. I also knew that JP had never left us. He'd only been trying to bring someone home.

FIANÇAILLES
THE ENGAGEMENT

"THERE WILL BE no tomorrow, not for JP and Flirt," Bonbon said.

Mr. Wilkes-Boggs gave up all pretense of respecting Bonbon's bereavement. "Madame, I am afraid that is unacceptable. We agreed to this *displacement* in exchange for a litter, and I intend to have one."

Bonbon smiled coyly. "You shall have your *portée*, your litter, Monsieur *Bog*," she said slowly, deliberately, and mostly in English, with particular emphasis on the truncated pronunciation of his name.

• • •

"But Flirt is a champion of the highest order!" Mr. Wilkes-Boggs said to his wife, avoiding all eye contact with me.

Bonbon had determined that JP had found his match, that it was true love, and that there would be a proper engagement. I was attempting to translate all this—and Bonbon's ways, her *originalité*, as Père called it—into a language the Wilkes-Boggses could understand.

"Of course she is," I said. "Anyone can see that. It's just that Madame Clix has certain other requirements for mating. She believes that a dog's instinct should be a part of the process."

Mr. Wilkes-Boggs didn't think this statement warranted a comment.

"Rupert, if Madame Clix prefers Marvella, what's the harm?" Mrs. Wilkes-Boggs said.

"The harm!" he cried. "The harm is that she is not *on heat*, and even if she were, she won't be two years old until October. More importantly, we've a bitch *on heat now*, a bitch this woman insisted we deliver to her personally at a decidedly southernmost point on the continent."

Mrs. Wilkes-Boggs nodded understandingly. "Yes, darling, but if the breeding *can't* happen."

"*Can't* happen!" he exclaimed.

Mrs. Wilkes-Boggs opened her hands to the air. "You saw the dogs as clearly as any of us."

"What I've seen," he now said to me directly, "is a fanatical woman who has no business breeding dogs! Indeed, what has become of Madam Clix's credentials? Other than an impotent stud, all I've seen are a ridiculously long genealogy and claims of champion stock! Where *are* the dogs she has been boasting about?"

•   •   •

"Of course Rupert won't admit it," Mrs. Wilkes-Boggs said, as Mr. Wilkes-Boggs tried to force JP and Marvella out of the pool by the palm tree where they were muddying themselves. "But Flirt is really my husband's baby. He adores her, and I think he's actually more miffed by JP's rejection of her than anything else." I had noticed how gentle he was with Flirt, and how focused Flirt was on him.

Mrs. Wilkes-Boggs had decidedly switched camps. She was moved by Bonbon's misfortune and her fight to reestablish *le domaine Clix*. Also, while Mr. Wilkes-Boggs favored Flirt, his wife had a preference for Marvella. In fact, she had been the one to choose Marvella to be Flirt's future replacement, but the dogs really belonged to her husband: Breeding was his life, not hers. She felt a bit guilty about it now, she said, because a dog needs a master, and Rupert had never really given Marvella the attention she needed. JP's interest in her obviously pleased Mrs. Wilkes-Boggs.

Mr. Wilkes-Boggs was less sympathetic, and he went so far as to imply that if Bonbon had loved her dogs so much, she should have looked after their safety better. I had described my first impression of *La Grange Canine*, Bonbon's barn, and how it was the most dog-friendly building I'd ever seen: Electrical outlets and cords were reinforced with indestructible rubber covers, and there were nonelectrical food and water dispensers with large reserves in case of emergency; it was as dogproof as any place could be.

•   •   •

Bonbon saw only the inevitability of the situation at hand, and seemed to genuinely believe that the opinion of the Wilkes-Boggses had no bearing. A decision had already been made by JP and Flirt. She saw the *inconvénient* of Mr. Wilkes-Boggs's *attitude*, of course, but it didn't deter her from sprucing up the Cabbage Patch for a *mariage de rêve*, even if the dream marriage wasn't to be consummated just yet. "Nature has taken its course," she said.

"And man is no match for Mother Nature," Père added with nuance.

"Madame has broken a nail and *Monsieur l'Abbé* has dirt under his!" Anna María shared her shocking observation while serving them *du citron pressé*, a testament to how hard they had worked uprooting unhealthy cabbage plants, replanting new sprouts, and giving the place an overall face-lift—yesterday's work on the Cabbage Patch might have been good enough for Flirt, but, Madame now realized, not for Marvella. She even scheduled a proper repair for the fence to replace our plastic patch job.

In the meantime JP and Marvella played in a field with a small pond where Bonbon's ass used to graze, under the supervision of Mrs. Wilkes-Boggs and me, and Mr. Wilkes-Boggs sought support for his argument—that Flirt was the fertile dog and the only one to be bred—from Dominique, who was at the *manoir* making a house call.

• • •

"What do you mean 'she's not ovulating'?" Mr. Wilkes-Boggs accused, although restraining himself since the mayor was a person of substance and authority, and a man.

"Well, not very much, she's not," Dominique said. "About ten percent, and in my *modeste opinion, Monsieur*, she is going *off heat*."

Mr. Wilkes-Boggs was stupefied. "I have been calculating the timing with utmost precision. How can this happen?"

Dominique shrugged a French shrug and sighed a French sigh. "*Ça arrive*," he said. "It could have been the *voyage*, the change in *climat*. It happens."

"God does not seem to be looking very favorably upon me at the moment," Mr. Wilkes-Boggs said to Père.

"Perhaps he is trying to tell you something," Père said in French.

"I'm sorry?" Mr. Wilkes-Boggs asked, irritated.

"God works in mysterious ways," I translated.

Bonbon decided to take a different tack. "*Monsieur*," she declared suddenly. "If you believe that I have financed your *vacances* in the south of France so that you could bring to me *une chienne* incapable of reproduction, you are *gravement* mistaken!"

Mrs. Wilkes-Boggs tried to stifle a laugh by covering her mouth. Bonbon winked at her. "Now please let's discuss the future engage—" Seeing that Mr. Wilkes-Boggs was beside himself with angst, she stopped herself from using that particular word. "—*arrangements*," she corrected.

Despite the fact that love had not blossomed in the Cabbage Patch, and a litter wasn't in the cards in the immediate future, Bonbon was infused with an almost childlike vitality that was both charming and hard to resist, even for Mr. Wilkes-Boggs. "If you wish to use our kennel's services, they will be rendered in Yorkshire," he suddenly said.

"*Quoi* ! What!" Bonbon exclaimed, pretending to misunderstand. "He wants that I marry him to a Yorkshire?"

"I am speaking of the county in the north of England, Madame," Mr. Wilkes-Boggs clarified, and Mrs. Wilkes-Boggs stifled another laugh.

Bonbon said she would make preparations for *une grande fête*, inviting "as many people as she could fit on *la grande terrasse* !"

A very distraught Anna María, who had, as usual, managed to overhear, suddenly materialized. "*Mais Madame*," she cried. "too many people is not good luck! It will make the dogs nervous!"

"*Ne vous inquiétez pas*, Anne-Marie, I just wanted to make sure you were listening. Hors d'oeuvres *only* . . . at eight."

"Eight!" Dominique said, exasperated. "*Ovulation, engagements, arrangements*. Why does it take you so long to have a party? I thought it was love we were here to *célébrer* !"

"There's one small matter to attend to before the celebration," Bonbon said.

•   •   •

"It is *hors de question*," Père said. "God does not recognize the marital union of animals. I thought you wanted a *mariage civil*, not a Catholic one. And I daresay that after what I witnessed at Escalet Beach with the Weimaraner, the husband will not be a faithful one."

Bonbon pouted. "Père," she said, imitating my way of addressing him. "It's all in fun—can't you please do it to humor me? Surely God wouldn't object to something that would *réchauffer* an old woman's heart?"

"Hauh!" Père exclaimed. "He'd have to plant another sun in the sky to be able to warm that heart!"

"Now Cyril," Bonbon said. "You know that's not true."

He smiled. "Yes, Bonbon, I do." He kissed her on the cheek. "And you're not old."

Père had two conditions. One was that the ceremony be attended only by family (and Dominique, who was already present and whom it would have been rude not to include; his presence was also useful because, after all, someone from the town hall must witness a civil marriage). The other was that because JP and Marvella weren't yet Catholic, they had to be baptized.

•   •   •

The sun was still bright in the sky and the cicadas were chanting when Père led the two dogs to the bench (which would serve as an altar) in the Cabbage Patch. Bonbon, Dominique, the Wilkes-Boggses, and I took our seats on the folding chairs that had been set up.

Unbeknownst to us, Père had dog treats hidden beneath his cassock, and so JP and Marvella sat obediently, unmoving, staring hopefully at him through two douses of the holy water

sprinkler. When the bride was asked if she took JP to be her husband, she was silent.

"Oh!" Bonbon exhaled, as if she had really expected her to
answer.

Mrs. Wilkes-Boggs was fast on her feet, however, and said,
"I'm terribly sorry, she doesn't understand French."

"Of course she doesn't!" Bonbon said.

Mrs. Wilkes-Boggs stepped up beside Père and said, "Now do
you want to marry this handsome man? Speak, Ella, speak!" And
Marvella spoke! "Good girl," Mrs. Wilkes-Boggs said.

"Good *idea*," Père whispered.

"Do you take Marvella, JP?" Père asked. "*Do you?*" he insisted, coaxingly.

After a moment of anticipation, JP pushed out a sound.

"I now pronounce you *chien et chienne*," Père said.

"It's official," said Dominique.

With that we all, even Mr. Wilkes-Boggs, showered JP and
Marvella with cold steamed rice as they chased each other fer-
vently through the Cabbage Patch.

CHIPS AND NEEDLES

"DOMINIQUE IS EXPECTING us this morning!" Bonbon shouted from my terrace. I didn't believe she would have made an appointment this time, and I would have ignored her had I not noticed that JP was, once again, not lying next to me. I jumped up.

"Don't worry, he's down here," Bonbon said, accurately imagining the scene. "I can hear him scratching at the door to get out to see me."

I made my way downstairs and stumbled over to open the door. JP ran out past Bonbon—but after a few feet, he reconsidered. He came back to give her a quick lick, and then bolted again toward the *manoir*.

"She's gone, JP," Bonbon said. He stopped, turned around, and lay down on the grass, looking depressed, hoping she'd notice and do something to rectify the situation. "But we are going to see *Merveille* this afternoon," she added. JP understood that Bonbon gave a French form to proper names whenever possible, and he knew who *Merveille* was. He bounced his tail off the ground a few times, jumped up, twirled, and then took a cold bath in the stream.

It was undeniably love between them. JP and Marvella had played for hours at *la réception* the night before, until they fell asleep on a sofa together, her head resting on his hip. When it was time to return to the mill, Mr. Wilkes-Boggs and I had to pull the two dogs apart, and I had bolted the door so that there would be no more visits to the village.

I had felt a bit sorry for Flirt, although she had seemed content to have the human attention all to herself. For the first time in her life she had been allowed on furniture, and for a while she had alternated between the laps of Mr. and Mrs. Wilkes-Boggs. I had a feeling that despite Mr. Wilkes-Boggs's inflexible exterior, the experience at *le domaine Clix* had changed him, and that Flirt's life would be better because of it. Mrs. Wilkes-Boggs had admitted to me that Flirt hated being pregnant and hated puppies—when I had asked her husband if they would breed her again, without hesitating, he said simply, "I think not."

"It's *Bog* who wants JP to see Dominique as soon as possible," Bonbon said when she saw my tired face. "Before he promises Marvella to JP, he wants to be certain that JP has the paperwork necessary for traveling to England. His blood must be tested, and then a microchip must be implanted—and there is a waiting period of six months before he can travel. This means that JP will not be able to travel in time for Marvella's next heat. Already *Bog* is not happy about that. He wants to breed her as soon as possible after she turns two in four months."

"Blood?" I looked at JP.

"*Oui*," Bonbon said. "Just a small vial to test it for rabies."

JP looked at me, and then disappeared under the table.

•　　•　　•

"*Superbe. Et merci*," Dominique said enthusiastically into the phone, and hung up. "It's a good thing you're late," he said to us.

"I'm sorry, Dominique, but His Highness went for a swim this morning and I know how you detest wet fur," Bonbon said.

JP had entered the clinic first, anxious, no doubt expecting to see Marvella. When he had searched every nook and cranny, he returned to Dominique's office and sighed.

"*Non, sérieusement,*" Dominique said. "I've some good news! I've just had a call from a patient who is not going to Scotland and won't need his microchip. This means we won't have to wait for the blood results—JP can have his chip today." Dominique produced a plastic bag containing a syringe with a very large needle.

JP knew what needles were, and didn't like them; he moved from beside Dominique's desk to behind me.

"That's good news?" I said, wondering just how big the microchip was.

"Yes, this way we can take the blood—and inject *this* today." He held up the bag so that I could see the encapsulated chip. It was the size of a small pebble.

"*D'accord, pépère,*" Dominique said to JP. "Blood first." JP sat still, seeming, to my surprise, not even to notice while Dominique pumped out a small vial's worth. "*Très bien,* good boy, JP," Dominique cooed.

JP gave an obligatory wag as if to say, *Em hmm.* Now *what?*

Bonbon inhaled as Dominique removed the other syringe from its plastic bag. "*Mon Dieu,*" she said. "Look at that thing! Why can't the English tattoo their dogs like everyone else?"

Dominique reminded her that French tattooing required dozens of needles, ink, and sometimes anesthesia. He found a good spot on JP's shoulder and rubbed alcohol onto it. "This won't hurt too much," he said.

As Dominique was injecting, Bonbon tried to comfort JP: "It's okay, we're going to see *Merveille* right after this."

Upon hearing her name, JP jumped up—just as the needle was going in. The three of us stared, openmouthed, at the needle, which was forced in all the way to the plastic handle. JP didn't bark, yelp, or cry. He simply keeled over on his side, out cold.

•   •   •

"*Il joue la comédie !*" Bonbon said. "That's all it is! An act." But it wasn't. JP had passed out, or worse. Dominique was so angry—and fearful—that he made us go to the waiting room while he administered an emergency treatment he didn't want us to see.

"*C'est de ma faute.* It's my fault. *Entièrement,*" Bonbon said, putting her head in her hands, and this time I was not inclined to disagree with her.

•   •   •

"*Ça va,*" Dominique said. "He was only unconscious ten seconds, fifteen at the most. We hit a nerve, that's all. I used some smelling salts—they woke him right up. His shoulder will be sore for a couple of days, and his nose might burn for an hour or so, but otherwise, *tout va bien*, all's well."

Bonbon was out of her seat in a flash. "Oh, thank God! Can I see him?" JP was already walking into the room. "*Mon bébé,*" Bonbon said, holding her arms out to him.

JP kept on walking, right past her and out the door, which was always left wide open for the sea breeze. He stopped and looked back at me, and only me. *Let's go*, he was saying.

"He's upset with me," Bonbon said in the car. JP was seated in the back, pressed against me, as far away from Bonbon as possible. He didn't stand to put his head out the window, he didn't do any licking, he just sulked—but he wanted me close to him, and for that I felt selfishly happy.

"You can't blame him, Bonbon," I said, still a little upset with her myself. "I mean, how would you have liked that thing stuck four inches into your back." She looked at me in the rearview mirror with a confounded expression.

"Don't be silly. He's not angry with me about *that*. He's angry because that's twice I've promised him he'd be seeing *Merveille*, and I haven't delivered," she said, a smile forming on her lips. Then, in a high-pitched voice, she pulled over to the side of the road, parked the car, and said, "But we're going to see *Merveille* now!"

JP jumped into the front seat, licked Bonbon across the face, and jumped out the open roof.

•　　•　　•

"*Il est là !*" Yvonne said as JP walked into the restaurant. "Look who's here!" He had raced from the car and up the steps, but as excited as he was, the instant he entered the building he remembered his manners, slowed to a walk, and waited for Bonbon and me.

"You see?" Bonbon said. "Dogs don't hold grudges. He doesn't even remember that little misadventure." I nodded and hoped she was right, since vaccinations were an annual occurrence. "But I suspect you and I will never forget it, will we?" she added softly. She always knew just the right way to offer an apology so that it was impossible to stay angry with her.

"I've put you over there today," Yvonne said to me, and kissed both of my cheeks. She pointed to a large corner table at the far end of the restaurant that faced a garden. Mr. Wilkes-Boggs and Marvella were already there. The two dogs spotted each other instantly, and I could see that Mr. Wilkes-Boggs had to hold Marvella back with one hand; with the other he waved to us, holding an engaged mobile phone.

JP, ever mindful of restaurant protocol, waited, albeit impatiently, for me to advance. Yvonne revealed a bone she had been hiding and discreetly handed it to JP. She then shook Bonbon's hand warmly, but offered no kiss.

"*Ça vous va ?*" Yvonne asked me, in case I wasn't satisfied with the table. I nodded and she winked.

"I'm not stupid," Bonbon said to me as we walked to the table. "I booked it under your name."

JP walked directly to Marvella and offered the bone to her. She delicately latched onto the other end, and then both dogs slipped underneath the table where they lay side by side, shoulders touching, to savor it. Mr. Wilkes-Boggs snapped his phone shut and stood up to greet us. Oddly affable, he kissed Bonbon on the cheek and shook my hand too hard. *"Bonjour, bonjour,"* he said, smiling broadly at his own French words, probably the first he had ever uttered.

"Hello," Bonbon said.

"And who do you suppose that was?" he asked Bonbon gleefully. Bonbon looked at me, not for a translation, which I now knew she didn't need, but because this was such odd behavior. Bonbon shrugged. "Mildred won't be joining us. I'm afraid she's feeling a bit under the weather."

"Hopefully it's nothing serious," Bonbon said in French, and I translated.

"Oh, thank you, no. Perhaps she's just not used to this glorious sunshine," he said. "But I'll tell you the good news—" Mr. Wilkes-Boggs stopped as Jean-Louis popped the cork of a bottle of 1995 Veuve Clicquot, and then paused, seemingly for effect.

"Oui ?" Bonbon said.

"My friend from La Garde-Freinet," he said, and paused again, to taste the champagne. "Em, lovely."

Jean-Louis filled our flutes.

"And your friend?" Bonbon prodded.

"Yes," he continued, "his wife is ill and he is returning to England."

Bonbon frowned. "And this is good news?"

Mr. Wilkes-Boggs stopped smiling. "No, of course not," he said, attempting solemnity. "But he must sell his house here, and he has made us a proposition we can't refuse!"

Bonbon sipped her champagne. "This is good news?" she said to me in French.

I held up my empty glass to Mr. Wilkes-Boggs's good fortune and translated. "That's wonderful news."

ADIEU

"Cash it," Père said of the check for three thousand euros that Bonbon had slipped under the back door of the mill. "She inherited all this on her wedding day"—he indicated *le domaine*—"along with an absolute fortune, so I'm told. What else has she got to spend it on?"

When he heard I was leaving, Père also tendered 910.62 euros in an envelope, which represented to the centime his share of the bill from Oustaù de Baumanière. "Sharing one's fortune, no matter how small or large, is a splendid thing that in the end will increase it," he went on. "That's just the way things work."

I pointed out that the money was technically a fee for a service not yet performed, and that in any case it wasn't exactly proportionate.

"Not yet performed!" Père exclaimed. "You're here, aren't you? And after all you've had to endure? Who's to say what your time is worth?" I couldn't think of too much I'd had to endure, unless he meant the near drowning and my run-in with Didier, but neither of those events was connected to Bonbon. "Everything is interconnected in this world, Gregory," Père said. "Don't imagine that it isn't. And don't believe for one second that receiving is any less important to one's spiritual well-being than offering—it's all part of the flow. Learn to accept with grace and just say *merci*."

I handed Père's envelope of cash back to him.

"*Merci*," he said.

• • •

"What are you talking about?" Bonbon said when I told her that I'd feel better accepting the check once the dogs had been bred. "That money is for the *débroussaillage*. I'd have paid a fortune to have that done professionally. And your travel expenses—of course I included a little something for the dinner in Les Baux—Père told me how much it cost, and I couldn't let you pay for our priest."

Bonbon had been strangely detached when I'd told her the previous evening that JP and I would be leaving today. There were two *non-nons* in French etiquette that had served me well in the past: Never be the last one to leave a dinner party; and no matter how gracious the host, never be a houseguest for more than a few days—not if you expect a future invitation. I'd already stayed ten days at the mill, and I wanted to be invited back.

But I found Bonbon's tone businesslike, as if she were embarrassed by my sudden desire to leave, perhaps because we had bonded on something other than a professional level. I felt sorry, and wasn't sure how to backtrack to the intimacy.

"It's not that I don't want to stay," I said to Bonbon.

I was surprised—and even a little hurt—when Bonbon interrupted me to say: "*Bien sûr*, it's time for you to go back to Paris." She busied herself with paperwork, something I'd never seen her do, and added with a polite smile: "Of course you'll be back. Maybe the breeding can even take place here, now that *Bog* will be a resident." She had never before referred to the deed as *breeding*.

"I hope JP and I can come back to visit before then!" I said.

Bonbon smiled but didn't look up from her papers. "*Oui*, if you'd like to."

"I was thinking possibly even in August, when Paris will be closed and I won't be able to work, anyway."

"That soon?" She looked up.

"I mean, we'd stay in a hotel," I said.

"You'll stay right here, *tous les deux*, the both of you," she said, and shoved her papers in a drawer.

• • •

"*Vive la France!*" Madame Poulin hailed as JP and I rode up to her house, and I feared that even her always open, American-friendly door might finally be closing as well.

"*Bonjour, Madame*," I said, in as perfect an accent as I could muster.

"*Bonjour, Madame !*" she cried. "*Qu'est-ce que c'est que cette histoire ?* What's the meaning of this *Madame* business? Have we gone all formal now that your daughter-in-law is English?" I was relieved, grateful that I hadn't inadvertently offended her, too. I hugged her, but I think in my heart I was probably hugging Bonbon.

Hugging is something the French rarely do among themselves, but they will tolerate it coming from foreigners, as long as they've reached an appropriate level of familiarity with them. Madame Poulin was thrilled, especially because JP was unable to resist joining in and managed to squeeze himself in between us.

"No, it's because we're leaving for Paris tonight and I have to remember my manners," I said. In Paris the *Madame* would never have been omitted when addressing a neighbor of Madame Poulin's age, no matter how friendly we had become.

Her face dropped. "I thought JP had fallen in love, and his girlfriend was moving to La Garde-Freinet."

I told her that the Wilkes-Boggses were only buying a vacation home, and that as far as I knew, the breeding would still take place in England.

"*Vive la France !*" she said to JP. "What's the matter? Is a French girl not good enough for you?" She shook her head and went to get some Swiss cheese.

•   •   •

"You won't believe it," Yvonne said. The restaurant was closed during the day while the employees cleaned and did the food prep, but I'd found her hosing down the front steps, no doubt cleansing them of dog pee. "The crazy butcher's wife just came by asking where she could find you!"

My departure from the Var *was* timely. "I hope you didn't tell her!" I said.

"Of course not." Yvonne turned off the water. "But she left something for you."

Aude had left us each a box of *nougat*, specialty taffy from Provence, along with a note apologizing for the *attaque* by her husband. Yvonne's box was open, with a small piece broken off.

Aude had explained that they'd been trying to wean her husband off his medication, but they'd apparently reduced it by too much. Yvonne looked doubtful when she was relating this to me.

"How can you measure insanity? He's crazy enough to think you'd fancy that horror of a wife, but sane enough to come after you with a rubber knife so he can't be put behind bars." I laughed because she was serious, and tore off a piece of *nougat*.

"What are you doing?" Yvonne asked, taking the candy from my hand. "Don't eat that! Who knows what's in it?"

I pointed to her box. "You've eaten some of yours."

She looked at her box. "The heck I have!" she said. "I made *her* eat that piece in front of me. Who's to say she's not a lunatic, too? *Ceux qui se rassemblent, s'assemblent*," she concluded. "Birds of a feather flock together."

And now that she'd considered the risk of poison, she'd be driving all the way to the Haut Var, the back country, every other day for the best meat.

• • •

"Good riddance!" I could hear Bonbon saying to Anna María. When she saw me standing in the doorway, she waved me over and told me *her version* of the news: The Wilkes-Boggses had hired Samuel out from right under Bonbon's nose to look after their new house while they were in England. "Can you imagine?"

I could imagine, since it was obvious that Bonbon and Samuel didn't suit each other. Samuel had often bragged that he had trained to be a butler and not a caretaker.

"Well he's *still* a *gardien*—who ever heard of a *French* butler?" And *who'd* want a stooge like Samuel for one anyway? Abandonment seems to have become a theme in my life." She sighed. "So, did you and JP enjoy your last morning in the village?" She looked at her watch. "Shouldn't you be pack—" She didn't finish her sentence, and I saw that her outburst was not a reaction to Samuel leaving at all—in fact, I think she was probably relieved to be rid of him. It was JP's and my departure that was upsetting her.

I told her that we'd be taking the night train from Fréjus to Paris—JP's ticket was half price, and the cost of transporting the scooter was cheaper than a couple of days' worth of gas. Also, it gave me some more time to say good-bye. Yvonne had proposed to open the restaurant for a private luncheon today.

"That should be *agréable* for you," Bonbon said.

"What, you're not going?" I asked.

"*Non*, I shouldn't. Am I expected to go?"

"I'll cancel if you don't," I said.

•   •   •

Before returning to *le domaine*, I made a detour to the Coteau Fleuri. The girls were already in the Range Rover, and Mr. and Mrs. Wilkes-Boggs were loading their suitcases, but they were as reluctant as I was to leave.

"Are you feeling better?" I asked Mrs. Wilkes-Boggs.

"Oh, yes, thank you. Actually, no, not really. I mean . . . it's lovely here, isn't it?" she said. "One just feels like exhaling—constantly."

I knew what she meant. It wasn't just the village, the Mediterranean, or even *le domaine*. It was all that, but it was also something more that had to do with the people. They didn't just get through the day, they *felt* life, absorbed it, every minute of every day, and so, by proximity, visitors had to as well. Even the less enjoyable minutes were refreshing.

JP had sat himself by the rear hatch of the Range Rover, and Mr. Wilkes-Boggs finally opened it to let him visit with Marvella. "Of course I was planning on stopping by so they could say good-bye," he said. He looked troubled. "Ahm, Greg." He cleared his throat. "Has ahm Madame—has Samuel told Madame that he proposed to come and work for us? We simply couldn't refuse." I congratulated them on their good fortune. First the house, now the new caretaker. I had another proposition I hoped they couldn't refuse.

•   •   •

Père arrived at the restaurant just as Bonbon, JP, and I pulled up on the scooter. "Oh my goodness," he said.

Bonbon smiled and lifted her leg over the scooter with surprising ease. "You thought I was too old for it?" she said.

"Not at all. But I'd have thought Madame Poulin was too old for Gregory. That woman has had my ear all morning—Gregory this, JP that, and *Vive l'Amérique* !" Bonbon and I laughed.

"Not *Vive la France* ?" I asked.

Père shook his head. "Not at all!" He imitated Madame Poulin's voice: "Not one of my Parisian neighbors has ever had the decency to say good-bye when *they* leave to return to the city, and it's not as if my door isn't always open!"

Before we went inside, I did something very un-French. "I want this to be a fun lunch, and so I want to say this now," I said. Bonbon and Père looked at me very seriously. "I need to go back to Paris. I have my life to straighten out and a job to find and—" Bonbon started to interrupt, possibly to offer me one, "—and a tree in my apartment that needs to be watered," I continued.

"Oh." Bonbon nodded.

"I don't live here. I'm just passing through."

"It doesn't feel like that, though, does it?" Père said.

I was trying not to get emotional, and to finish whatever it was I was trying to say and unfortunately hadn't scripted. "I'm so sad to be leaving you that I—it's why I'm taking the train, so that once I'm on it, I won't be able to turn back." JP came close, leaned against my leg, and looked up at me.

"So I haven't driven the two of you up the wall?" Bonbon asked.

"You've changed the way I look at life," I said, and JP sidled up to her. Père said nothing, and therefore something.

Bonbon took my arm as we walked up the steps. JP entered first. Les Santons, in his eyes, was losing its restaurant status and becoming merely his dining room. The chef greeted us, holding his hand out first to Père because of his priestly status, and then to Bonbon. JP walked across the dining room and over to the kitchen door, where he began to scratch. I called him and he came crawling, begrudgingly, one inch at a time, constantly looking back in the direction of the kitchen.

"Something must smell good," Bonbon said. "It's *très aimable* of you to open for us."

"It was either that or miss saying good-bye," the chef said jovially, leaning down to rub JP's ears. JP looked back at the kitchen. "Don't worry, *pépère*, your risotto is coming."

·   ·   ·

Dominique was late, and so Yvonne served us the *apéritif maison*, a blackberry *kir, pour passer le temps.*

"You can order from the *carte*—or you can let the chef surprise you, since today seems to be a day for surprises," Yvonne said, looking at me with mock admonishment. "In any case, it's on the house."

Bonbon shook her head. "Oh no, I couldn't let you do that."

Yvonne placed menus on the table and left, saying that we were not to pay for the meal and that was that.

"*Apprenez à recevoir*, Bonbon," Père said. "Learn to accept."

JP started moving around under the table, constantly repositioning himself, until he finally came out completely from behind the tablecloth and sat beside Bonbon.

"He's *agité* because he doesn't want you to take him away," Bonbon said. JP looked at her pleadingly, and whined. "You see?"

There was a strange scraping noise coming from the kitchen.

Yvonne emerged, back first, through the heavy swinging door, as if struggling to close it behind her.

"Gregory, *je suis désolée*, but knowing Dominique, it could be *hours* before he gets here. This is torture!" she said.

"Dominique is here, *ma puce*," Dominique said, entering the door.

"Ah *voilà*," Yvonne said, and at that instant the kitchen door started to vibrate. "Ah *voilà*," Yvonne said again, and the door was opened several inches—just enough for Marvella to pry her way through.

JP leapt up from the table and the two dogs met halfway across the salon, overturning a chair. They licked and pawed and wrestled. Nothing existed for the two of them except each other, not even the two platters of risotto the chef brought out and set by our table.

"Okay, JP," I said, "*à table*." As if Marvella, too, now understood French, both dogs settled in under the table and snuggled tranquilly.

"*Quelle joie*," Bonbon said, marveling at the love between JP and Marvella. "*Où sont les Boggs ?*"

"On their way back to England," I said.

Bonbon, Père, and Dominique looked at me to explain more, until finally Père, understanding, cracked a smile. "Bonbon," he said.

"Gregory—" Bonbon said.

I interrupted her: "Thank you for JP." I cajoled Marvella out from under the table and said, "*Marvella, dis bonjour à ta maîtresse.*" Instinctively, she did as she was told and stretched herself up to kiss Bonbon, and then she kissed me. Bonbon said nothing, but she shook her head over and over, dazedly.

"I'd better get the smelling salts," Dominique said. We all laughed, even Bonbon, as tears began to stream down her face. JP and Marvella were back under the table, their legs intertwined. "*Là, là !* Behave yourselves," Dominique said to them. "Don't forget! No funny business until she's two!"

Yvonne returned with a camera. "I've got to get a shot of this," she said. She snapped one and Bonbon screamed "*Non !*" because she didn't want her mascara-stained face to be on film. Hearing her *maîtresse*, Marvella popped her head out from under the table and looked at Bonbon questioningly, to make sure everything was all right.

"*Quelle beauté,*" Bonbon said.

"Oh," Yvonne said. "I almost forgot." She produced an envelope and set it on the table. "An Englishman asked me to give this to you. He said to tell you it wasn't necessary."

Bonbon reached for it, and extracted its contents—it was her check to me, which I had signed over to Mr. Wilkes-Boggs as payment for Marvella. She pressed the check to her heart, and then tucked it into my shirt pocket.

There is *a God,* I thought.

G4 9/09
Bc 1/10
P.C 5/10
BKM9/16
Mc 1/11
RlL 5/11

TILLAMOOK, ORE.
COUNTY LIBRARY
1-09